MORE SERMON~

BIBLICAL ~

Rev. CLOVIS (

Be

, oy Drive,

Belfast BT5 6 BB.

MORE SERMONS ON
BIBLICAL CHARACTERS

BY

CLOVIS G. CHAPPELL

BAKER BOOK HOUSE
Grand Rapids, Michigan

Reprinted 1971 by
Baker Book House Company

ISBN: 0-8010-2327-0

Reprinted from the original
printing made in 1923 by
George H. Doran Company, New York

CONTENTS

MORE SERMONS ON
BIBLICAL CHARACTERS

MORE SERMONS ON BIBLICAL CHARACTERS

I

THE PRODIGAL WIFE—GOMER

Hosea 6:6

"Mercy have I desired and not sacrifice." George Adams Smith translates this: "Leal love have I desired and not sacrifice." My story is one of the most pathetic ever told. It is a tragedy of the parsonage. It tells of a preacher's broken heart and of a preacher's broken home. The guise in which this terrible calamity came was the worst possible. It came through the unfaithfulness of the preacher's wife. Gomer might have been the happiest woman in Samaria. To her much was given. From her much was expected. But she turned away from her possible paradise to plunge into a pigsty.

The scene is the city of Samaria. Jeroboam II is king, and the era is one of great prosperity. It is also one of luxury and of debauchery and of open and disgusting vice. Society is becoming more and more rotten. Ten years before Amos had spoken in frank and awful plainness of coming ruin. But Samaria had not heeded. It had continued on its downward way as if greedy for its own destruction.

Now it was in this city that Hosea lived and preached. He was a man deeply patriotic and genuinely religious. He had the vision of a poet and the devotion of a saint. It was here he met and loved a girl named Gomer. She was in, and, doubtless, of this flippant and wicked society of Samaria. How he came to meet her and to fall in love with her we are not told. It is very evident, however, that to this love he brought the unsquandered treasure of a strong man's heart. Hosea had never sacrificed on the wayside altar. He had therefore much to give. Gomer responded in some fashion to his love. Doubtless her clay soul glowed for a little while under the spell of its warmth. At least she consented to become his wife. Thus this brilliant and gifted young preacher was married. And according to his own convictions there was every promise of highest happiness.

Of course we are aware of the fact that a man usually finds his heaven or his hell in the woman that he marries. Hosea did not find his heaven. He found his hell. Gomer did not sympathize with him in his work as he had expected. This patriotic young preacher was doing his utmost to save his people from national disaster. He had constantly in his ears "the rumblings of a nation that was falling to pieces." He knew that the war chariots in Assyria, whose coming meant utter ruin, were on the point of being set in motion. He must call Israel back to God if she is to be saved. Therefore he was giving himself with all earnestness to the work of the ministry.

But Gomer did not care for these things. She had no sympathy with what to her seemed the wild and unpractical dreams of her too spiritual husband. She only fretted and felt piqued that he gave so much time and attention to these high matters. She threw it in his face with petulant tears when he came home at night that he cared more for his preaching than he did for her. She began to tell herself and to let others tell her that she was leading a starved life; that she was young and pretty and made for enjoyment; that she had, therefore, a right to an existence that was fuller of romance and of gaudy colors.

For this reason the young preacher lay awake at nights sometimes longer than was good for him. For this reason he often went about his duties with knit brows and with a heavy weight upon his heart. He did not acknowledge it to himself, but he was keenly disappointed. He saw that there was a chasm widening between him and the woman that he so passionately loved. And being the man that he was he could not look upon this widening chasm without the bitterest of secret pain.

Then it was that an event took place in the little parsonage home that brought great joy. At least it was a great joy to the young husband. The sweet angel of suffering came and there was a little baby boy in the home. As Hosea held his firstborn in his arms he dreamed that a new and better day had dawned for him and his wayward young wife. He was conscious of the fact that she had had too many frivolous interests outside her own home. He remembered with pain that she did not seem to greatly enjoy his company. She was much more pleased with gayer society. But all this would be over now. This little fellow would put his baby hands on both their hearts and draw them closer together than they had ever been before.

But here again the young preacher was destined to be disappointed. Gomer did not become more devoted to her husband and to her home, but less so. Day by day the gay life about her seemed to more and more absorb her. Her husband, her baby, her home, were so many barriers between her and her rightful enjoyment. The young husband, in spite of his love and his cleanliness of mind, was becoming suspicious. At last with the passing of the years two other children were born, a girl and a boy. The one he named "Unpitied" or "Unloved." And the other he named "No Kin of Mine," for by that time he had a suspicion that amounted to a damning certainty that his wife was unfaithful to him and that the children born in his own home, born under his own roof, were not his own.

Then followed days of growing estrangement, with here and there a period of reconciliation. Gomer would weep her passing sorrow upon his heart and then go back to her old life. Her repentance was like a morning cloud. It was soon past and gone. At last there came a dark day when Hosea returned to find the children alone in the nursery. Possibly there was a tablet left in the hands of Jezreel. It read something like this: "You need not seek me. I will never come back. I have gone away with another who promises to make me happy. I have determined to live my own life."

It was a terrible blow. In fact it was the worst possible blow. No greater wound ever comes to man or woman than that. There is a new tenderness in the father's touch as he mothers the three children that night. He hears them say their prayers, teaching them possibly a new petition: "God bless mother and bring her back home."

Then the children slept, but there was no sleep for

the deserted husband and father. Back and forth he paces, pausing now and then to look into the faces of the sleeping children. He gazes with a special heart-hunger into the face of the little girl. She has no resemblance to himself. But she is so like her mother; her mother's eyes; her mother's tangled curly hair. Is that a strong man's sobbing we hear? And is this what he is saying: "Oh, Gomer, how can I give thee up?"

Thus the night passed. Then there was a day equally bitter. Then many nights and many days crept by on leaden feet; nights in which there were no stars and days in which there was no sun. And Hosea struggled under the weight of his awful agony. He stood painfully questioning with God about this bitter and terrible tragedy. As last his eyes became clear to see and his heart wise to understand. His very tears became telescopes through which he looked deeper into the heart of Infinite Love than any other man of his day. Over this path of pitch Hosea was led into a knowledge of the Gospel deeper, possibly, than that of any other man in the Old Testament.

What were some of the lessons that Hosea learned through this awful tragedy? First he learned something of the nature and meaning of sin. As he brooded over the unfaithfulness of Gomer, as he thought of her desertion, as he broke his heart over her going from his own home, he came to realize that as Gomer had sinned against him, so had Israel, the bride of Jehovah, sinned against God. The sin of Gomer was unfaithfulness. The sin of Israel was also unfaithfulness.

Not that Gomer's sin consisted in the mere fact that she deserted himself and his home and gave herself to another. He learned that sin was something more than an outward act. It was an inward something. It was a thing of the heart. It was a perversion of the will. Gomer did not begin to be unfaithful when she left his home. That was only the end, the outward expression of an infidelity that had been begun months and years before.

How had this terrible domestic tragedy begun? It had begun in Gomer's heart. She began by losing sympathy for her husband. She ceased to appreciate his purposes and his plans and his ideals. She came little by little to think that life with him would be a lean and mean and starved affair. She seriously mistrusted his ability to bring her real happiness.

Then she began naturally to seek her happiness elsewhere. She said: "I am young. I have but one life to live. I have a right to enjoyment. I have a right," as we are so fond of saying today, "to live my own life." And when I hear anybody say that I know that the individual who says it is preparing to do something that is selfish and wicked. For to claim that you have a right to live your own life is nothing more nor less than to claim that you have a right to do as you please. It was thus that Gomer ceased to trust and love her husband and gave her confidence and her love to another.

Her sin against her husband, therefore, was not simply in the fact that she left him. She might have sinned against him little less and remained in his home. Many husbands and wives today who live in the same house and face each other daily at their meals are just as wide apart as were Hosea and Gomer. They have ceased to be bound together by the only bonds that can bind a husband and wife together, and those are the bonds of love and confidence. Where these do not exist, whatever else may be present, there is no real happiness and no real wedded life.

And what is it to sin against God? Is it to lie or to steal or to commit murder? These are only the out-workings of sin. They are the symptoms of an inner rottenness. To sin against God is to refuse to trust Him, to refuse to give Him your allegiance, your loyalty and your love. It is to turn from finding your happiness and your joy in Him to seek them else-where. It is to refuse to make His will supreme in order that you may be wrecked by the kingship of your own will.

Now this sin may express itself in far different ways. One man may reject God in order to waste his substance in riotous living. Another man may reject Him in order to lead a life that is altogether decent and moral and respectable. Why did the Prodigal Son go into the far country? Because he wanted to; because he sought to please himself rather than to please his father. Why did the Elder Son remain at home? For the same reason. Sin therefore is not so much the outward act as it is an inner disloyalty of the heart.

Just as sin in its essence is a thing of the heart, just so, also, is true religion. What did Hosea want of Gomer? Did his heartache over her going mean only that he missed her service about the house? Did he grieve over her unfaithfulness because when she was gone there was no one to sweep the floors and dust the furniture and prepare the meals? Would he have been satisfied had she hired a housekeeper to take her place in that deserted home? A million times no.

What Hosea wanted was not a drudge. He wanted a wife. That is, he wanted a companion. He wanted one who could enter into loving sympathy and fellowship with himself. And that is what God wants. "Leal love," He says, "have I desired and not sacrifice." He is not asking for your service primarily. He is not asking for your money first. He is asking for you. His appeal is ever this: "Son, give me thine heart." If He gets that He gets everything. If He does not get that He gets nothing at all.

The next lesson that came to Hosea through this sordid tragedy was a realization of God's grief over man's sin. How did he learn this lesson? He learned it through his own grief. Hosea could not see Gomer becoming daily more flippant and frivolous, daily more and more coarsened without grieving over her. It broke his heart to see her love for the filthy and for the unclean. He could not take her going away as a trivial thing. Daily and nightly on her wandering way poured a mourner's tears.

Why was this so? It was true for the simple reason that he loved Gomer. In spite of her sin he loved her. And because he loved her he could not but suffer, he could not but grieve, he could not but break his heart as he saw her turn from himself to cling to the thing that he knew would work her ruin. And so God was grieving over Israel. And so God is grieving over you and me. Sin always means pain. It means pain to the sinner. Oftentimes it means pain to those nearest to us. Always it means pain to the heart of God.

"And he beheld the city and wept over it, and said, If thou, even thou, had known at least in this thy day the things that belong to thy peace." There is something terribly startling in that picture. Whose is that tear-wet face? It is the face of Jesus Christ. It is

the face of Him in whom dwells all the fullness of
the Godhead. It is the face of Him who said, "He
that hath seen me hath seen the Father." Therefore,
our God is a God who grieves. His face is everlastingly wet with tears; tears over your sin; tears over
my sin; tears over the sin of the world. Hosea grieved
over the sin of his wayward wife. God grieves over
the sin of His wayward people. And His grief is as
much greater than the grief of Hosea as His love is
greater than that of Hosea. He is a God infinite in
love. Therefore He is a God infinite in grief.

Finally, Hosea learned through this terrible experience something of the amazing mercy of God. It is
easy to guess how he came to this discovery. To the
amazement of himself, to the greater amazement and
even to the disgust, doubtless, of his friends, he had
never been able to cease to love his unfaithful wife.
Gomer had despised him. She had wronged him in the
worst way that she could possibly have wronged him.
She had made him an object of scorn among his enemies
and pity among his friends. She had dragged his
good name into the very gutter. She had seemed to
utterly forget him. But though he was forgotten he
could never forget.

I can well imagine the many grim battles that he
had with himself. The story has just come to him
of a recent chapter in his wife's sordid life. He hears
of her doings of last night, of the wild night in some
brothel. And the friend who tells him said, "I suppose you will divorce her now. I suppose you will turn
from her forever." And he makes up his mind to do
just that. Alone he tries to blot out her memory and
to tear her image forever from his heart. But he cannot do it. Though the foul breath of passion has blown

her like a filthy rag out of his arms and out of his home it is a part of his hell that he loves her still.

Then he is led to think of God. God is infinitely better and infinitely more loving than himself. If he has been unable to divorce Gomer, if he has been unable to forget her though she has forgotten him is not God's heart quite as tender as his own? Hosea knows that it is infinitely more so. So he comes to realize something of that love that will not let us go. He comes to appreciate and to understand the reality of that love about which John spoke when he said, "For God so loved the world that he gave his only begotten son that whosoever believed on him should not perish, but have everlasting life."

Then one day a terrible piece of news comes to this sensitive and fine-souled preacher. He hears that the man who has lured his wife from him and who promised to make her happy has deserted her. Worse still he learns that he had sold her. That princely knight that promised so much, that told her of the great happiness to which he was going to introduce her was only a "white-slaver" after all. Coming with the promises of large freedom he brought in reality only binding fetters and galling chains.

It is the history of sin through all the centuries. It makes wonderful promises but it never keeps them. "If you will sin you will be as God," said the Tempter to the woman at the beginning of human history. And so she made the venture, expecting to find a fuller and freer life. But she found that the promise that was made to her was only a cheat, it was only a devil's life. So will you find it. So has every one found it since history began.

I know that to some a life of righteousness looks

cramped and narrow. I know the life of sin looks free and broad. There are so many more things that the worldling can do than the saint is privileged to do. But did you ever realize that there are many things that the saint can do that the worldling cannot? And these are the big things. The saint can pray and believe in God and be useful. And that the worldling cannot. But still we allow ourselves to be humbugged. We seek the freedom that sin offers and find, alas, that it is slavery and nothing more.

If all who have found this to be their actual experience were to say "Amen" at this moment it would boom like an earthquake and shake like a cannonade. Ask Samson if this is not the case. He broke away from the restraint of Israel. He must taste life. He must enjoy some bit of freedom. But the end of it all was blinded eyes and fetters of brass and grinding in the prison house. Ask Gomer. She must have the bright lights. She must have the flattery and fawning of many admirers. But now the lights have all gone out and she wears a chain, a slave in the filthiest of all filthy slave markets.

What a deceiver is sin. How true is that sentence in Revelation: "The hair of a woman," that is charming, lovely, fascinating to look upon, "and the teeth of a lion," powerful to fascinate, powerful also to tear, to enslave, to destroy, to damn. There is a spider, I am told, that is quite flowerlike in appearance. But the bee that comes seeking honey finds itself gripped by the tentacles of death. There is also a spider called sin. Oftentimes it is fascinating in appearance, but its touch is slavery and its grip is destruction.

"May I speak to you?" a friend might have said to Hosea one day. And they conversed together in low tones. "You say she was sold last night to the highest bidder?" and the prophet's eyes are big with unshed tears and his face is tense and drawn with pain. "Yes," was the reply, "she was sold last night. Surely now you will get a divorce. Surely you will turn from her for evermore, and blot her name utterly out of the book of your remembrance." "I will try," is the low answer. "I will try, but I do not know."

But that very night Hosea slipped away from the children a little while. And when they followed him to the door and asked him where he was going he hesitated and then kissed them all again and said: "I am going to bring mother home." And he goes, not to a home of purity, but down into the haunts of shame. He goes to pick up this bit of human wreckage called Gomer that the seething seas of sin seem to have spit up upon the shore. He buys her from her owner for fifteen pieces of silver and a homer and a half of barley, and brings her home again.

What happens after this we do not know. The curtain is dropped on the pathetic and ugly tragedy. It is possible that the love and devotion of this good man may have softened Gomer's heart. Maybe she repented. Maybe she wept her way back to God. Maybe she became a good woman. Maybe she heard a voice saying to her: "Though your sins be as scarlet, they shall be as white as snow." But I fear that she did not. I fear that to the last she rejected his love. I fear that to the end of the day she was as much an outcast in the home that was once hers as she was in the far country.

For though love is the mightiest thing in the world it is possible to resist it and to reject it. It is possible to resist and to reject human love. It is possible to resist and reject the love of God. To many it seemed little short of madness for this pure and good man to so love his wayward and sinning wife as to go to the slave market and buy her and give her another chance. In the presence of such a love they stood amazed and bewildered.

But here is a far more wonderful story. When you and I had resisted and insulted the love of God, when you and I had turned from Him in cool contempt, when we and all our brothers had made shipwreck in so doing, our Lord did not utterly cast us off. In His mercy He refused to throw us away. But He came also to the slave market and bought us back. The price that He paid was not fifteen pieces of silver and a homer and a half of barley. The price that He paid was His own life. "For even the Son of man came not to be ministered unto, but to minister, and to give His life a ransom for many. . . . He was wounded for our transgressions, He was bruised for our iniquities: the chastisement of our peace was upon Him, and with His stripes we are healed." Will you respond to that sacrificial love? Will you cast yourself in helpless penitence into His arms? If you will He will make you whiter than snow. If you refuse, yours is the unpardonable sin, for it is the sin against love.

II

A FULL MAN—STEPHEN

Acts 6: 8

During the busy and eventful weeks immediately
following the day of Pentecost, people separated by
wide chasms were brought into the fold of the Christian
brotherhood. Among this number were foreign-born
Jews and home-born Jews. These had hated each other
heartily in the past, but now they were being welded
together by the bonds of their common faith in Jesus
Christ. This growing spirit of brotherliness, however,
was not permitted to continue without hindrance.
Something took place at the time of our story that
came very near splitting the infant Church into angry
and opposing factions.

The cause of this unfortunate situation was this:
many of the recent converts to Christianity were not
allowed to return home. They were cut off from all
financial support. They stood face to face with pinch-
ing poverty. To meet the demand for immediate help,
big-hearted men came forward, such as Barnabas, who
gave their all to the support of these needy and home-
less converts. The funds thus obtained were put into
the hands of the Apostles and were administered by
them.

But for some reason the administration of the Twelve
did not prove satisfactory. The foreign-born Jews became convinced that they were not getting a square
deal. They claimed that their widows were neglected

in the daily ministration. Then it was that the Apostles very wisely decided to remedy the evil by a further organization of the Church. They saw that they themselves had been undertaking too much. They realized that they had been giving their time and their energies to a much needed work, but to a work to which they were not especially and divinely called.

For this reason Peter and his fellow Apostles came before the multitude with this wise suggestion: "It is not reason that we should leave the word of God, and serve tables. Therefore, look ye out among you seven men full of the Holy Spirit and wisdom, whom we may appoint over this business. But we will give ourselves continually to prayer and to the ministry of the word." That was an exceedingly wise decision. And great is the pity that all ministers of the Gospel have not exercised the same high and holy wisdom.

You see that these Apostles were in danger of being side-tracked. They were in danger of giving all their time to work to which they had not been appointed. Had they done so, they must needs have lost much of their effectiveness in their own divinely appointed work. And the danger that they faced and avoided is one that has only grown greater with the passing of the years. In our day the machinery of the Church has been greatly multiplied. Preachers are better trained today than they have ever been before. But I am afraid that the modern Church, with all its weak spots, is weakest in its pulpit. We as ministers have become skilled in many ways, but we have done so at a great price. Too often we have lost our skill at doing the supreme things. We have forgotten how to "give ourselves continually to prayer and the ministry of the Word."

When the multitude heard the suggestion of Peter

and his fellow Apostles, they greeted it with hearty welcome. And it is my opinion that there was at least one name that was immediately suggested to almost every man and woman that was then present. "They are going to select seven men to administer the temporal affairs of the Church? Then I know one who is just exactly fitted to be president of that committee. I know one who is exactly the man to be Chairman of the Official Board." So one of the listeners said to his neighbor. And the neighbor answered immediately: "Yes, I thought of him the instant that Brother Peter made the suggestion. You are thinking of our young brother, Stephen, no doubt." And so he was and so was almost everybody else. Thus Stephen was chosen and was made president. And I have a fancy that his election was unanimous.

Now it is with real pleasure that I introduce to you this morning Stephen, Chairman of the Official Board. This ancient lay preacher is one of the most charming personalities in all the history of the Church. His whole story is told in two chapters of the New Testament. We watch him live for but one brief day of his life. We see him pass early and swiftly. But he abides long enough to leave his name written indelibly upon our minds and hearts. He appeals to us as embodying in himself the very highest and kingliest qualities of Christian manhood.

Doctor Luke's admiration for this gifted young man is very evident. He has one word that he applies to him again and again, and that is the word "full." In the estimation of Luke, there was a fine well-roundedness, a fascinating fullness about Stephen. He did not impress Luke as being a fractional man. He was not a one-sided, half-baked individual. He was well-rounded, full-orbed. He was finely balanced, well grown. He impresses his biographer as one the elements of whose character were so mixed that nature might stand and say to all the world, "This is a man."

Stephen—full. But what is the next word? In what did Stephen's fullness consist? That is a supremely important question. There are some full folks that we cannot away with. We say, "I could like him, but he is so full of himself. He is so full of irony. He is so full of sarcasm. He is so full of trickery and treachery." There are some people who repel us because their souls are peopled with varied and unattractive demons.

But what of Stephen? "Stephen, full of faith." That is the first fine element of his fullness. He was a man not with a meager and timid and invalid faith. He was a man not with a sickly little handful of faith. He was a man full of faith, so full that though doubt came and knocked at his door every morning and every noon and every night, Stephen simply smiled and shook his head and said, "No room. Faith is my guest now." "Stephen, full of faith."

That means, of course, that Stephen was on good terms with God. That means that God delighted in Stephen and that Stephen delighted in God. That means that there was a fine intimacy between them, an intimacy that can exist in no other way. "For without faith it is impossible to please God. For he that cometh to God must believe that He is and that He is a rewarder of them that diligently seek Him."

Not only was Stephen full of faith toward God. He was also full of faith toward men. It does not take a wise man to see why this is true. How do we know that Stephen trusted people? How do we know that

he believed in folks? Here is positive proof: folks
believed in him. The whole brotherhood regarded him
with fine firm trust and confidence. And cynics and
misanthropes are never so trusted. If you put a question after everybody's name, do not forget that they
will put that same kind of mark after yours. But faith
begets faith.

Not only was Stephen full of faith, but he was full
of wisdom. "The children of this world," said Jesus,
"are wiser in their generation than the children of
light." Yes, that is true, but Stephen is a lovely excep-
tion. Stephen had that faith that could see visions
and dream dreams, but he was more than a dreamer.
He was a man of hard-headed common sense. He was
a man who brought those faculties that would have
made him a leader in the world of finance or of politics
and dedicated them fully upon the altar of his Lord.

"Stephen, full of wisdom." If there were hard questions about the administration of the Church they consulted Stephen. He was always ready with a suggestion that showed the keen insight of genius. If there
was an individual with perplexities and problems with
which he did not know how to cope, he came and talked
with Brother Stephen about them. Though young in
years he was wise. He was so wise that the keen
historian Luke, writing under the inspiration of the
Holy Spirit, said that he was "full of wisdom."

"Stephen, full of power." If there was a fine virtue
that he seemed to be more full of than any other it is
this of power. Where Stephen went, things happened.
Changes took place, revolutions were wrought, and it
stands written in the Record, "they were not able to
resist the spirit and the wisdom by which he spake."
He was full of power. The word used for power here

is the one from which we get our modern word, "dyna-mite." This young saint was full of moral dynamite. He was a spiritual tornado. He swept things before him with an irresistible force.

Full of power—that is not the word that we may use about the Church as a whole in this day of grace. Full of power—that is not the way we would go about describing most of the church members that we know. Full of power—that is not even the word that we would use to describe the majority of our ministers. Full of eloquence, it may be; full of learning; full of fine and gentlemanly qualities; full of a thousand desirable char-acteristics. But full of power—that is a description that, sad to say, describes only the few.

And yet was there ever a day when powerful saints were any more needed? Were they ever more needed in the pulpit and were they ever more needed in the pew? I know we have decency and respectability and kindness of heart. We have money and culture and social standing. But power—do we possess that abso-lute essential? "Mount Vernon Place Church, full of power." Is that the way our church is entered upon the books of Heaven? Is that a fit description of us as individuals? Surely it ought to be. Surely our oppositions are terrific enough to make power an abso-lute necessity. And yet we must realize that the word "full of weakness" would be a far better description of too many of us.

But, for our consolation and encouragement, let us bear in mind that this fine fullness may be ours. "Full of power" may as fitly describe you and me as it did Stephen of this far-off day. He who made men mighty centuries ago makes them mighty still wherever and whenever He has His way. "Ye shall receive power,"

He is saying to us at this moment. "Tarry ye till ye be endued with power." Oh, believe me, if our Christianity is the Christianity of the New Testament, it is a mighty something. It is a force in the presence of which the thunders of Niagara and the sweep of tornadoes will be as weak and trifling things.

Then there is one more fullness that Luke ascribed to Stephen. "Stephen, full of grace." And when you hear that you recall that bejeweled sentence from John's Gospel: "And the Word became flesh and dwelt among us, full of grace . . ." Christ was full of grace. Christ's servant Stephen was also full of grace. That is, he was charming. He was magnetic. He was fascinating. He was attractive.

"Stephen, full of grace." He cast a spell over folks. He was as winsome as the springtime; as attractive as sea music. When folks were in his presence, they found themselves strangely comforted and helped. The broken-hearted forgot to sob when he was by. The hopeless forgot their despair. The wounded forgot their hurts. The barren and desert-hearted began to dream that the dreary wastes within their own souls might be made to rejoice and blossom as a rose. He was a gracious man.

And yet he did not win men merely to himself. What says that bright star yonder that keeps eternal lids apart in the night sky? It says, "I owe my charm to another. I would have no beauty except it were given me. For me to shine is the sun." And so Stephen, full of grace, spoke to men of a gracious Savior. As they went away from listening to him they said, "I will go and learn something of his charm. I will go and consult the same Specialist that he has

consulted, and see if He cannot smooth the care lines
and the frown lines and the sin scars out of my own
face."

"Stephen, full of grace." And that grace spoke in
every tone of his voice. It looked out through his
kindly eyes. It shone in every lineament of his face.
"And they saw his face," the Record says, "as it had
been the face of an angel." Truly he had found the
secret of real beauty. Ho, every one that thirsteth for
real charm, every one that longs to be genuinely and
truly attractive, come and sit at the feet of the young
preacher Stephen. He can show you how to become
winsome with the very winsomeness of Jesus. He can
show you how to lay hold on that which many of us
lack so much and long for so much. He can show us
how to be full of grace, full of charm, such grace and
charm as cannot but be a blessing to the whole circle,
whether large or small, that we are privileged to touch.

But you say, "That is well enough for Stephen living
in the very shadow of Pentecost. But it is not possible
for me. It is easy enough for Stephen to be full of
these fine graces. But I have no hope personally of
any such fullness. If I even make a start in that
direction my life is soon depleted of its energies. All
my moral forces are soon exhausted. Therefore, I see
no hope for myself either for today or for tomorrow."

But before you reach this dismal conclusion, let us ask
the secret of Stephen's fullness. What is the secret of
the continued fullness of our old home spring down in
Tennessee? It is not the fact that that spring never
gives out any water. It is not the fact that no one ever
stoops to drink its laughing life. It is giving, giving,
giving all the time. Indeed it would exhaust itself in

less than an hour but for one fact. It is fed from hidden and inexhaustible sources. Far back in the heart of the great hills is a reservoir that can give from generation to generation and never be exhausted.

And this is Stephen's secret. He is a greatly gifted young man. I am aware of that fact. There was not another man in the Church in his day who had his ability. He had an intellect that in its wide and daring grasp of things was a rival to that of St. Paul. But this does not account for him. Neither is he accounted for by saying that he was a well-trained, a finely cultured young man.

What, then, is the secret? How comes he to be full of all the fine graces that we have mentioned? These are but the natural outcome of another fullness. It is mentioned by Luke in the very beginning and accounts for all else. Listen: "Stephen full of the Holy Ghost." Here then is the spring from which all these rivers flow. Here then is the sun that lighted all these winsome stars. You can only account for Stephen's graces and fine enviable qualities by saying that he was a man in whom Christ dwelt in the person of the Holy Ghost.

And surely this blessed fullness is just as much within reach of you and of me today as it was within reach of Stephen. "Jesus Christ is the same yesterday, today and forever." What He did, He does. Wherever He has been able to get possession of men as he got possession of Stephen He begets those same high qualities. Oh, may we not this day, because of the needs of our own lives, because of the needs of our homes, because of the needs of our church, offer ourselves fully to Him. He waits to be gracious. He waits to enter in and possess us. For "we are His witnesses as is also the Holy Ghost, whom God hath given to them that obey Him."

And look a moment at the outcome of this fullness. "Stephen, full of the Holy Spirit, and therefore full of faith and wisdom and power and grace." But what was the end of it all? What did it amount to? The first result of this fullness was not simply that he was a joyous and sunny Christian. He was that. But what we want to notice especially is the effect of his fullness upon the world, upon the people of his own day and the people of all days that have come and are to come after.

Stephen, then, full of the Holy Spirit was full of highest usefulness. He was appointed to a position that looked quite small. He was to help administer the temporal affairs of a semi-pauper Church. But he made these temporal affairs to administer to highest spiritual ends. He gave out bread in such a fashion as to make men hunger for the Bread of Life. And when he passed out a bit of money to the needy he did not forget to tell them where they could buy wine and milk without money and without price. He worked with his might in his small sphere and God honored him and made him a mighty preacher.

And how effective he was in his preaching. Jerusalem was a proud and wicked city. It was full of cultured and religious aristocrats. Those aristocrats would have given a world to have been able to ignore Stephen. Nothing would have suited them better than to have been able to treat him with cool and complete contempt. But they could not ignore him. They might as well have tried to ignore a burning building when the wind was high. They might as well have tried to ignore a cyclone. There was hardly a man in Jeru-

salem stupid enough and sleepy enough not to know
that Stephen was in town on a business trip for his
King.

Mark you, I do not say that everybody welcomed
Stephen's message. I do not say that everybody who
heard him repented and became a follower of Jesus
Christ. Many did. Many even among the priests
yielded to his impassioned appeals. Many hearts were
softened. But this was not true of all. Some were
made only the more bitter. Some had all the serpents
within their souls awakened into activity. Some were
led to hate him with a hatred that only his life blood
could satisfy. But this I say, they could not remain
stupidly and stolidly indifferent.

And do I not voice the longing of your heart this
morning when I say, Oh, for a Church that the world
cannot treat with indifference. Oh, for a band of saints
that it is absolutely impossible to ignore. Oh, for a
ministry that will divide audiences and communities
and cities and continents into those who are either out
and out for Christ or out and out against Him. Oh,
for a Christianity virile enough to compel the active
opposition, the open antagonism of the forces of evil
that refuse to be won. The Church of Jesus Christ
can stand any amount of opposition. "The gates of
hell shall not prevail against it." But the direst of all
dire calamities is for it to become so effete, so powerless,
so dead, that it is not worth fighting.

Stephen, full of the Spirit, I repeat, became Stephen,
full of highest service. Where he labored many fell in
love with his Lord. Where he labored opposition grew
bitter. His enemies ground their teeth like enraged
beasts. But Stephen with a fine high courage continued
his message. He went on with his sermon, though he

knew that every sentence that he uttered was becoming a stone in the hands of his enemies. He spoke right on though he knew that he was digging his own grave as he spoke. "Ye stiff-necked and uncircumcised in heart and ears, ye do always resist the Holy Ghost; as your fathers did, so do ye."

The assembly becomes a mob. The young preacher is hurried out of the city. The scene that follows is nothing more than a common lynching. These men have not been able to resist his inspired logic. They have been publicly humiliated. They will have their revenge. And so they pelt him with stones. His angelic face becomes bruised and blood-stained. A few minutes later he lies battered and broken and very still. And the wolves have had their prey.

But they had not been able, with all their stones, to kill his open vision. "I see the heavens open," he cries, "and Jesus standing at the right hand of God." Though they killed his body they were not able to kill his Christlike spirit of forgiveness. As he falls a victim to their hate he throws around their cruel shoulders "the sheltering folds of a protecting prayer": "Lord, lay not this sin to their charge." Though they killed his body they were not able to destroy his peace. "Be quiet," says the mother, as she puts her baby to sleep. But God can put his child to sleep amidst the howl of mobs and the flying of stones. And so Stephen fell asleep.

Stephen, full of the Holy Ghost, was a blessing while he lived. An abiding blessing he has been through all the changing years. One young man stood by that day well pleased with his death. But he was never able to banish the picture of the angelic face of this first Christian martyr from his mind and heart. At last this proud man fell prostrate on the desert sand with this cry upon his lips, "Lord, what wilt thou have me to do?" And I feel confident that the first of the saints that Paul greeted when he reached the heavenly country was "Stephen, a man full of the Holy Ghost."

III

THE PAINTED FACE—JEZEBEL

2 Kings 9: 30, 31

Hear the text: "When Jehu was come to Jezreel, Jezebel heard of it; and she painted her face, and tired her head, and looked out at a window. And as Jehu entered in at the gate, she said, Had Zimri peace, who slew his master?" This face at the window gripped the attention of Jehu at once. It held the fascinated attention of every man with him. No man could pass this face by and utterly ignore it. It was far too striking, too arresting for that.

Now of course Jezebel was not striking simply because her face was painted. The painting of the face was quite a common thing in that day. It was fairly prevalent among the American Indians. It is even sometimes practiced among ourselves by the exceedingly bleached and the exceedingly young. So far as I know it is quite an innocent form of disfigurement. It is also at times quite perplexing. Why a young girl, for instance, with the fresh roses of youth upon her cheeks, would take pains to hide these lovely flowers under a glaring coat of artificiality, is beyond my comprehension. But so she often does. However we are interested neither in the young girl nor in Jezebel because of her paint.

As we get a glimpse of the face of this woman, Jezebel, we cannot fail to recognize something of its coarseness and cruelty. In the springtime of life she may have been a beautiful girl. But that is passed now. Years of sinning have left their ugly marks and scars upon her and no skill of painting can wholly hide them. In fact any outward adornment is ever a poor substitute for the loss of inner loveliness. When the hot blasts of iniquity have withered the fair flowers of the soul there is little to be gained by trying to reproduce them outwardly upon the cheeks.

But if this painted face of Jezebel is striking for its cruelty, it is no less striking for its strength and intelligence. Jezebel is capable and forceful. She is the worst hated woman in the Bible. That alone implies strength. We do not hate weaklings and pigmies. We hate giants. Jehu calls her the "cursed woman." She is the evil genius of her day. She is the Lady Macbeth of the Old Testament. She has all the ambition and all the brilliant, dashing courage of that illstarred queen. She also has all her flinty cruelty and stoniness of heart. Surely Lady Macbeth's prayer was answered in full on behalf of Jezebel.

> ". . . Come, you ministering spirits
> That tend on mortal thoughts, unsex me here,
> And fill me from the crown to the toe top-full
> Of direst cruelty! make thick my blood;
> Stop up the access and passage to remorse,
> That no compunctious visitings of nature
> Shake my fell purpose, nor keep peace between
> The effect and it! Come to my woman's breasts
> And take my milk for gall, you murthering ministers,
> Wherever in your sightless substances
> You wait on nature's mischief! Come, thick night,
> And pall thee in the dunnest smoke of hell,
> That my keen knife see not the wound it makes,
> Nor heaven peep through the blanket of the dark
> To cry, 'Hold, hold!' . . ."

Here then is a woman whose name has become a synonym for all that is basest and most bloody. Here is a woman whose life ended in direst and ghastliest tragedy. And every one feels that it should have been so. Every one must feel that in dying as she died she was but reaping as she had sown. But how did she come to be the monster that she was? How did Jezebel come to be a name to make us shudder? It was not always an ugly name. There was a time when a queen mother and a father who was king thought it a fit name for a beautiful and tender baby girl. How do we account for Jezebel?

Now, there is one easy way to account for her and that is to say that she was born a monster. We love to think, as others have pointed out, that those people who go greatly wrong are made of different material from that of which we ourselves are made. We love to think of them as constructed of the slime and ooze of things, while we ourselves are composed of much finer and purer material. But in so thinking we are wrong. We are wrong for the simple reason that no child ever comes into the world wholly bad. I know it means much to be well born. I know that some children do not have as good opportunity in this respect as others. But no child is ever a monster from the beginning.

So what Jezebel became was not altogether a result of bad birth. "Every child comes into the world with the kiss of a loving Father upon its innocent soul." And there is not one single stain upon the whiteness of its little heart. It has the possibilities of descending into the depths. But it also has the possibilities of ascending into the highest heights. The path it takes is determined in some measure by its heredity. We are conscious of that. But it is determined in far greater measure by its teachers.

The supreme cause of the moral failure of Jezebel, I think, was that she was born in a heathen palace and had an early training that was bad. She was nurtured in an atmosphere that was foul and filthy. She was trained in a religion that infected its votaries with moral leprosy. The gods to whom she was introduced were gods of filth and lust. They were mere dumb symbols of iniquity that neither had nor claimed the slightest power to make men good. They neither had nor claimed the slightest longing to make men good.

As was perfectly natural, this early training cast its blight over Jezebel's entire life. It is hard indeed to get over a wrong training in childhood. It is possible, through the good grace of God, to do so. But it is very rare indeed that those wrongly trained avail themselves of that possibility. Of those who come into our churches, of those who even attend our churches, the overwhelming majority are the ones who had some sort of religious training in youth. In my entire ministry I never recall to have seen one single man or woman converted who had not in some fashion been brought into contact with the teachings of the Gospel in their young and tender years.

Then Jezebel had a second handicap. She made an unfortunate marriage. Her husband, you remember, was named Ahab. Ahab was nominally a follower of the Lord. But in reality his religion counted for naked nothing. The big difference between him and the woman he married was that while he was weak and and wicked she was strong and wicked. If Ahab had been a man of true and vital faith, if he had been strong through the power of God, he might have saved his gifted queen and through her he might have gone far towards saving the nation. But she dominated him and turned him to her religion, instead of him turning her to his.

Yes, Jezebel dominated her weak husband and turned him away from the faith of his fathers. A woman seems naturally stronger in this particular than a man. We meet thousands of women who are loyal and consecrated and conscientious Christians and whose husbands are utterly indifferent or even antagonistic. And yet these faithful and brave and loyal hearts hold on their course, year after year, undaunted and unconquered. But how rare it is to find a man, even a strong man, who will hold on his way when his wife is out of sympathy with him. I have seen a little butterfly of a society girl, whose weight morally was about that of a bubble, quench the zeal of a strong man. I have seen her turn him away both from his church and from his Lord.

Not only did Jezebel influence her husband and dominate him, but she did the court the same way. And dominating the court she also dominated the nation. She hated the religion of the Jews. It was narrow. So with profound audacity and a daring that would have been commendable in a noble cause, she displaced it with the corrupt and corrupting religion of her own nation.

How much the world missed by this woman's failing to be a good woman. What a zealous worker she was in the interest of religion that she knew to be altogether vicious and rotten. She was so active and aggressive and enthusiastic that she fairly swept the nation off its feet. After a few years of her zealous propaganda we find a faithful preacher saying to God: "For the children of Israel have forsaken thy covenant, thrown down thine altars, and slain thy prophets with the sword; and I, even I only, am left; and they seek my life, to take it away."

You will remind me, doubtless, that Elijah was mistaken. You are correct. He was. God said: "There are seven thousand that have not bowed the knee to Baal." And yet what a pitiful little handful this was in a whole nation that claimed loyalty to Jehovah. Jezebel was a worker and she worked successfully. It is true that the gospel that she preached was a gospel of filth and degradation. It is true that her message was a message that had in it the germs of an eating cancer. But notwithstanding the poorness, yea, the utter hellishness, of the story that she had to tell, she told it with a fiery zeal and courage that produced most tragic results.

And here are we, followers of Jesus Christ. We claim Him as our Lord, of whom it is said, "The zeal for thy house hath eaten me up." He has entrusted us with His Gospel, which Gospel is the power of God unto salvation. We have a story to tell that is the one hope of this perplexed and groping world. And yet how feeble we are, how listless, how indifferent, how stupid. Oh, for more souls on fire both in pulpit and in pew. If we had as much zeal and enthusiasm in the preaching of our gospel of salvation as did this woman in the preaching of her gospel of lies, we would turn the world upside down.

The third cause that contributed to the ruin of Jezebel was her prosperity in wrong doing. She was stronger than her husband. She was stronger than the people about her. She sinned openly and above board. And the more she sinned the stronger she seemed to become. She became the dupe and victim of successful sin. Success in any enterprise is more or less dangerous. But the most ghastly and damning of all success is success in sin. The man who is sorely wounded in his first encounter with evil may come to hate it and turn away from it. But the one who prospers in wrongdoing is in great danger of becoming permanently married to the thing that will mean his utter ruin.

But God did not leave Himself without a witness even in that far-off day. Jezebel cannot rise up in judgment and claim that she had no opportunity. She had all the light that she needed for the guidance of her feet from the paths of ruin into paths of blessedness and peace. Her pastor was one of the big and brawny and broad-shouldered sons of God of the Old Testament. He was one of the greatest men that ever came to speak for God in this world. When Jesus was here, he was one of the two sent from heaven to talk to Him about the mystery of the Cross. She had Elijah for her preacher.

Now, no one could come into contact with Elijah and ever be the same. Elijah was "incarnate conscience." A certain woman in whose home he was for a time a guest said to him: "You have come to bring my sin to remembrance." He did not tell this woman that she was a sinner. By being what he was he made her conscious of what she was. One man said of a certain preacher that he never saw him even pass along the road that he did not make him sorry for his sin and hungry for a better life.

Gypsy Smith was preaching in Paris some years ago. At the close of one of his services cards were handed out for those present to sign who desired to become

Christians. One of the cards was signed by a young princess of the house of Bourbon. Gypsy Smith had been speaking in English and this young princess did not understand English. Therefore her companion expressed surprise and said: "Why, you did not understand a word that he said." "I know I did not," was the reply, "but I could tell by the very tone of his voice and by the look of his face that he has something that I need." Gypsy Smith was an incarnate conscience. And so is every man just in proportion as he lives in the fellowship of Jesus Christ.

Now this man Elijah came into the royal palace one day and said to the guilty pair: "There shall not be rain or dew upon the earth except at my word." And the fountains of Israel dried up and the grass grew sere. And the flowers faded and the leaves withered. And Israel became a desert, sentinelled by death. What was the matter with Israel? Ahab knew and Jezebel knew. It was sin that had cut off Israel's water supply. That is what has changed your heart garden into a desert. You have tried to think that it is because you have not achieved your ambition. Or because you have suffered this loss. But when you dare look yourself eye to eye and be perfectly honest, you know what the trouble is. You know what is your tragedy. It is just this: it is your sin. It is the miserable quarrel of your soul with God.

Jezebel knew what was the matter. So did Ahab. But they were not willing to face the facts. When Elijah comes back after three and a half years of drouth, Ahab goes to meet him. He is bearing in his mouth, I feel confident, the question that Jezebel has taught him: "Art thou he that troubleth Israel?" And how prompt and true is the answer of God's prophet:

"I have not troubled Israel; but thou, and thy father's house, in that ye have forsaken the commandments of the Lord."

But these royal sinners of long ago preferred to blame the rebuker of their sin instead of the sin itself. They blamed the physician rather than the disease. They desired to use the knife upon the surgeon rather than upon their own festering rottenness. And their kind is not dead. There are still those who try to make getting angry at the preacher a substitute for repentance. There are those still who seek to cure their deadly diseases by showing the doctor the door.

Just the other day I read how insanity had doubled in Chicago in the last two years. The reason given for this appalling increase was the vast amount of vicious bootleg liquor that the people were drinking. And the moral drawn was this, that the Eighteenth Amendment ought to be repealed. That is, the law written into the Constitution of the United States is responsible for the drunkenness of those people in Chicago. Now is that true? Nothing could be more untrue. It is not the law that made them drunk. It was a flagrant violation of the law. Get angry at the violation instead of at the law. Blame the sin that has turned your garden into desert rather than the prophet who warns and rebukes you. To take the opposite course is madness.

It was not, therefore, lack of light that was the ruin of Jezebel. If this experience had not been enough there were others. Jezebel knew all about that heroic test on Carmel. She knew the failure of her own gods. She knew how the God of Elijah had answered by fire. Then later she had been made to realize how the sin of Ahab had found him out. It had come very close to her when her husband, who had consented to Naboth's murder, was himself fed to the dogs by the pool of Samaria.

But Jezebel was not softened. She was made the harder. Not that she did not believe in the reality of God. Not that she did not believe that sin had horrible consequences. But she shut her eyes to these facts. God gave her all the light she needed, but she deliberately refused to give hospitality to the light. Thus she came to that ruinous position where she believed that God's law worked in every case except her own. She believed that sin would find the sinner out provided that sinner was not herself. She became convinced that the evil that would dethrone others would put a crown upon her brow. Thus she forged for herself her chains of doom.

And now she is facing the last act in the ugly tragedy of her life. The man who is to be the instrument of her death is entering in at the city gate. But this woman does not hide. She does not put on sackcloth and come before him to beg his mercy. She decks herself like a queen and stands in the window as a preacher of righteousness. And she hurls at her antagonist this question: "Had Zimri peace, who slew his master?" What does she mean by that question? She is calling Jehu's attention to the fact that when Zimri murdered his master his sin found him out. Zimri paid the penalty in a very few short days. And what she means is just this: "Jehu, be sure your sin will find you out. Jehu, whatsoever a man soweth, that shall he also reap."

Did she believe that? She believed it for everybody but herself. For a lifetime she had been sowing to the flesh. For a lifetime she had been sowing the seeds of lust and hate and murder. And all the while she had been flattering herself that she could reap a harvest that was altogether different. But she became then and there an illustration of her own text. "Who is on my side?" shouts Jehu from the street below as he looks at the painted face in the window. Two or three men show their faces. "Throw her down" is the order.

Do you hear the scuffling in that upper room? Do you hear that wild shriek, that dull thud? And there is a spattering of blood upon the wall of the building and upon the hoofs of the horses and the wheels of the chariot as Jehu drives ruthlessly over this woman whose life has been one long sowing of the seeds of iniquity.

Jehu enters into the palace and feasts himself. When the feast is over he bethinks him of the betrampled corpse in the street. And he says to the servants, "She is a king's daughter. Go out and bury her." But when they go out to gather up the remains, all that is left is a ghastly skull and the soles of her feet and the palms of her hands. And as I look at the hideous sight I can see one of those dog-gnawed hands write this sentence on the crimsoned cobblestones: "Be not deceived. God is not mocked, for whatsoever a man soweth, that shall he also reap."

And the thought that I cannot get away from is this: How differently this story might have ended; what a lost power for good was this brilliant and gifted woman. She gave her immense energies to sin and was the means of corrupting almost an entire nation. Had she given herself with the same dauntless courage and enthusiasm to God she might have been the means of the salvation of a nation, and future centuries would have risen up and called her blessed.

Oh, the power we throw away! I have looked upon great rivers rushing on their way to the sea, that turn few wheels and contribute little or nothing to the running of the world's machinery. I have seen Niagaras spending themselves in thunder. But the most terrible waste that God or men ever beheld is the waste of human life. Oh, the possibilities that are locked in the hearts and the lives of you that are listening to me at this moment. And yet some of you are going to squander your treasure. You are going to throw yourselves away.

"What are you going to do with yourself, Jezebel? You are brilliant, you are strong, you are capable, you are highly gifted. You have all a woman's personal magnetism and charm. What are you going to do with it all? How are you going to invest this God-given wealth?" Had Jezebel known the future as we know her life today and had she been honest, she would have answered after this fashion: "I am going to use my immense powers for the ruin of my home. I am going to make my husband into a murderer. I am going to stain the blood of my children so that by and by my sins will be visited upon them. I am going to take this body of mine and throw it out into the street for dog meat."

What are you going to do with your life? Are you going to lend it to that which makes for your own ruin and for the ruin of those about you? Remember that as you sow, so shall you reap. Sow to the flesh and you will of the flesh reap corruption. There is no avoiding that fact. It will work in your case. It will work in mine. The law of gravitation acts as ruthlessly with a prince as with a pauper. And so does the law of moral retribution. If you sow to the flesh you will of the flesh reap corruption. If you sow tares, tares will be your harvest. But if on the other hand you sow to the spirit, you will reap a spiritual harvest. Thorns will grow in this world and so will roses. Nettles will spring up if you plant them. Violets and honeysuckles will do the same. The field is yours. It is up to you to determine the harvest.

IV

COMING BY NIGHT—NICODEMUS

John 3:2

Hear the text: "There was a man of the Pharisees named Nicodemus, a ruler of the Jews. The same came to Jesus by night." Now, that was an astonishing thing for Nicodemus to do. It was amazing because of who this man was. Did you notice that he was a ruler of the Jews? He was a man then of position, and the One to whom he went had no position. He was an aristocrat and the man to whom he went was of the people. He was a man of the schools. He was a scholar, but the One to whom he went had no diploma. He had never won a single degree. He had never been inside a university. Nicodemus was a man who had got far on into life. His hair was white. He was now an old man, old in honor and in years. And the One to whom he went was a young man, young enough to be his son.

Yet we read this striking sentence: "The same came to Jesus." That one short word speaks volumes. It tells us a wonderful story about this ancient Pharisee. It gives us a marvelous insight into his character. When we read that about him we are interested at once because we know that the man who came to Jesus under the circumstances under which Nicodemus came was no ordinary man.

What sort of man was he? His coming indicates, in the first place, that he was a man with an open mind.

He was a man who was willing to learn. He was a man who would not let his prejudice blind his eyes to the truth. All the other men of his class condemned Christ without having heard Him. They decided at once that they did not care to believe that He was the Messiah, and not wanting to believe it, they refused to believe it.

It is easy to close our minds to the truth that we do not care to accept. It is so easy to shut our eyes to that which we do not wish to see. It is so easy to stop our ears to a message that we do not want to hear. And this is just as dangerous as it is easy. For the man who refuses to hear the truth loses his capacity to know. There is endless hope for any man, however late his start, if he is only willing to know. Another calls attention to the fact that George J. Romanes once wrote a book called "A Candid Examination of Theism." He decided against theism. He reached the conclusion that there was no God. But his work had this one virtue, it was candid. Romanes was willing to learn, and there came a time when he reversed himself absolutely and became a devout follower of Jesus Christ.

One time a gentleman came to a man by the name of Nathaniel and said to him, "We have found the man of whom Moses, the law and the prophets did write, Jesus of Nazareth." And Nathaniel looked at him in amazement and said: "Did I understand you to say Jesus of Nazareth? You cannot mean that the Messiah came from that despised town. 'Can any good thing come out of Nazareth?' "

And the man who had brought him the message did not argue with him. He said to him: "Come and see. Try it out." And this man Nathaniel was a fair-minded man. He did put the information that he had received to the test and he found it true. He found that even from despised Nazareth there had come one who was at once the Lord of his own life and also of Heaven and earth.

It may be that you are not a Christian. It may be that you have a prejudice against Christianity. It may be that that prejudice is founded upon a foundation as unreasonable as that upon which the prejudice of Nathaniel was founded. You may have been offended by those so-called followers of Jesus who have misrepresented Him. You may have suffered at the hands of one who belonged to the church. But instead of letting that blind you, suppose you be fair enough and candid enough to come to Jesus Himself. That is what Nicodemus did. Others of his class had condemned Him unheard. He said, "Before I condemn Him at least I will hear what He has to say. I will meet Him face to face. I will know what He claims and what He teaches." And so this candid and honest man came to Jesus.

His coming, in the second place, indicates a man who is in earnest. Nicodemus is a very serious man. There is nothing chaffy about him. He is not a mere human bubble. He is not a man who is capable of being satisfied with the doctrine of eating and drinking and being merry. He is very serious, very genuinely in earnest, very determined to know the truth and to follow it if he can find out what the truth is.

And mark me, the virtue of genuine earnestness is no mean virtue. This is especially true if you are in earnest about something that is worth while. It is the earnest man who wins his way to God. It is the earnest man who captures life's real prizes. To be flippant, half-hearted, lukewarm is to surely fail to reach any worthy goal. It is also to be disgusting both to man and to God. "Because you are lukewarm and neither hot nor cold I am about to vomit you out of my mouth."

Then, in the third place, he is a man of a splendid type of courage. I know that that is not the fact about him that is usually emphasized. The opposite is almost always set in the limelight. We are very fond of lambasting the timidity, the cowardice of this man. We point out sometimes with sorrow and sometimes with zest the fact that he came to Jesus by night. And we get so interested in that phrase "by night," that we forget what comes ahead of it.

The big fact is not that this man came by night. The big fact, the blessed fact, is that he came at all. There was much to hinder him. There were many things in the way, but in spite of all these hindrances, in spite of all obstacles, he did come. You may laugh at his cowardice. You may smile in scorn as you see him stealing along in the shadows. But I wonder if you who laugh have ever had the courage to come to Jesus even in the night. He may not have come with the open boldness that compels our admiration. But no fault of his manner of coming can obscure the blessed fact that he arrived.

He came to Jesus by night. That is true. I agree that the fact that he came in the night shows that he was a bit timid. I think Nicodemus was afraid. I think every footstep that he heard that night startled him. I dare say that he felt himself go hot and cold as he passed one whom he knew and from whom he feared recognition. He was afraid, horribly afraid. And yet he came. Do not forget that. And that shows a very fine type of courage.

There are two types of courage. There are men who have never felt fear. There are men that would not recognize fear should they meet it on the street. They simply are utter strangers to it. They never have and never will make its acquaintance. I have a friend of that type. He revels in danger. He glories in a fight. He never seems quite so happy as when he is likely at any time to be assassinated. For this reason he performs even his most dangerous duty with consummate ease. But there is another type of courage that I think even more admirable. That is the courage of the man who is naturally a coward. It is the courage of the soldier whose knees were shaking under him and who told those knees that they would shake more than that if they knew where he was going to take them in a few minutes. I honor the man who with a bulldog fearlessness never knows what it is to feel his knees go weak. But I honor still more the man who does the thing that he feels that he ought to do in spite of the fact that fear is clutching at his heart, that his knees are a-tremble and that goose flesh is creeping all over him. Nicodemus had that fine type of courage, the courage that even enabled him to go to Jesus in spite of the fact that he was horribly afraid.

The fact that Nicodemus came to Jesus showed, in the fourth place, that he was a heart-hungry man. Nicodemus was religious, but his religion had never satisfied him. He had given his life to the church, but the church had not quenched the deep thirsts of his soul. Somehow after almost a whole lifetime spent in the holy atmosphere of the Temple in the Holy City he was troubled and weary and dissatisfied.

He had been in some measure restless and disappointed possibly for years, but his dissatisfaction had been deepened by his acquaintance with Jesus. He had doubtless heard this young Rabbi on the streets of Jerusalem. His words had affected him strangely. They had given him a longing that was at once a pain and a promise. He felt that here was a man that knew a secret that he did not know. Here was one who though far younger than himself had wisdom that he himself had not learned. And so I see him urged on by his own burning thirst. I see him, lured by the hope that this thirst may be met by the young Prophet from Nazareth, making his way through the night to the humble abode of Jesus.

Now frankly I am interested in the errand of this man. I am profoundly interested in it because I find myself close kin to Nicodemus. I, too, have hungers and thirsts that no earthly power can satisfy. I have needs that no human soul can meet. Possibly they can be met in Jesus. I am sure they cannot be met elsewhere. And even though I may not be sure that He can meet them, yet I am going to give Himself and myself the advantage of the doubt and make a trial.

For this reason I am going to steal along in the wake of this night visitor. I am going to do this not that I may spy upon him; I am going to do it not that I may surprise him at his interview with the Young Carpenter and report him to the Pharisees. I am going to do it because my own heart is hungry. For this reason I am going to slip in through the door with him and share his pew in this night service and hear the marvelous sermon that he heard.

Brother, suppose you go in with me. Let us slip in and sit beside this great teacher and listen as he listened to a sermon from the Greatest of all Teachers. It is a wonderful privilege. Nicodemus never forgot that interview. He never could forget it. He shouts over it yet around the steps of the Throne.

There is a timid knock at the door. There is a movement on the inside, the quiet, stately steps of One who has heard the knocking. He comes, opens the door, and Nicodemus stands face to face with Jesus Christ, the Savior of the world. There were many things in the heart of this white-haired teacher that he wanted to ask Jesus. There was much that he wanted to say. He begins with the one big fact of which he is sure. "We know," he says, "that thou art a teacher come from God." Here is one who knows the mind and heart of God. And before Nicodemus can tell Him what the matter is, Jesus Christ has answered his question, not the question of his lips, but the question of his heart.

What did He say to this man who had dared to come to Him through the night? He did not say to him, "Nicodemus, I know what the trouble is with you; you are not honest. Nicodemus, you must quit swearing. Nicodemus, you must quit Sabbath-breaking. You must quit breaking your marriage vows. You must stop yielding to the lusts of the flesh." No, He did not say that to this master in Israel. Had he done so Nicodemus would have blazed upon Him, for he was guilty of none of these things. He was a clean man, a moral man, a religious man.

But what Jesus did say was this: "You must be born again." He said, "I know what is the matter. You have been trying to find peace and rest and joy and salvation by doctoring the outside of life. You have found that your well is poisonous and you have tried to remedy it by painting the well curb. You have found that the clock of life does not keep good time and you have spent endless care polishing the hands.

You have found the fountain of the heart sending forth a bitter stream and you have tried to remedy it by pulling up a few weeds that grew round about it. Nicodemus, you must be put right at heart. That is first. That is fundamental."

So Jesus declared to this pious and earnest and honest man the one supreme and universal necessity, and that is the necessity of a new birth. And remember that Jesus said this not to an outcast. He said this not to one who had wasted his substance with riotous living. He said it to one of the most cultured and refined and decent and religious men of his day. To this man's heart and conscience He spoke home and said, "You must be born again."

And I wonder if you feel disposed to resent this message. I wonder if you think that it is no longer necessary. I wonder if you think that it is old fashioned and out of date. Remember that it is Jesus who spoke this message. Remember these words fell from the lips of Him in whom dwells all the fullness of the Godhead bodily. And what He said to this man, and to all men, is this: "You must be born again."

And when Jesus said that He not only stated man's supreme necessity. He stated man's supreme privilege. What a pity it is that we read this as if it were some terrible sentence of doom pronounced against us. "Ye must be born again"—and we look at it and say, "Alas and alas!" Why is it? Is it because your old life has been so marvelously beautiful and so eminently satisfactory? Do you shrink from this doctrine because you are perfectly confident that you have already found the highest? Why not look upon it as your supreme privilege instead of something to be feared and hated?

Christ told Nicodemus that it was his privilege to be

born again. He told him that life might be made over for him even though he was old. That is marvelous indeed. I know of nothing, not even the resurrection from the dead, that is so wonderful as that a man may be raised into spiritual life who in time past was dead in trespasses and in sin. And that this is a possibility is a fact that has been proven over and over again millions of times. There is no experiment in chemistry that has been any more clearly demonstrated than the power of God to remake men has been demonstrated.

The new birth has been experienced by the most depraved and abandoned of men. It has been experienced no less radically by the most decent and moral. How do you account for the marvelous change that was wrought in Saul of Tarsus as he went that day from Jerusalem to Damascus? He was not a rake. He was clean and upright and dead in earnest. And yet there came to him an experience that utterly revolutionized him, and in the power of that experience he changed the history of the world.

Here is another man. He is a scholar. He is enthusiastic. He is brave. He becomes a missionary and buries himself in the wilds of America in an effort to convert the Indians. But he goes home a confessed failure. He preaches in England and declares that he preached much but saw little results. And then one night he does trust Christ, and Christ alone for salvation. And he comes forth from that service to bring England to a new birth. So whoever you are tonight, I preach to you this marvelous gospel, that your supreme necessity, your supreme possibility is a new birth. You must, you may be born again.

The sermon startled Nicodemus. It made him afraid. "How can these things be?" he said, in utter perplexity.

And as if in answer, the wind soughs around the corner. And Jesus said, "Do you hear the wind? 'It bloweth where it listeth and thou hearest the sound thereof, but canst not tell whence it cometh, and whither it goeth; so is every one that is born of the Spirit.'" You cannot see the wind, but you can experience it. You can know it for a strong and vital fact. And while you cannot understand all the mysteries of a new birth, you can understand enough to experience it. For while God's part may be far beyond your comprehension, your part is simple enough for the understanding of a little child.

How is it? "As Moses lifted up the serpent in the wilderness, even so must the Son of Man be lifted up that whosoever believeth in Him should not perish, but have everlasting life." We are reborn through faith in Jesus Christ. Leave off your speculations. Leave off your theories and accept this glorious gospel in its sweet simplicity. Do that and here and now you will experience what Nicodemus experienced and what countless multitudes that no man can number have experienced since then. You, too, will be born anew.

Nicodemus was never the same after this night. He went out to become a follower of Jesus. He was still a timid follower for many days. But when his colleagues condemned Jesus he dared speak in His defence. It was not as bold a speech as we might have desired, but he stood for Him none the less. He had become his friend. And when Jesus died, then at last he came out into full and acknowledged discipleship. And Christ finally succeeded in making the coward into a hero.

Just so Christ can remake you and me. Have you ever given Him the opportunity? Have you been born

again, born from above? Have you experienced that
change that is so revolutionary as to be called a passing
out of death into life? Have you so become a partaker
of the divine nature that you are not committing sin?
Are you in the power of this new life overcoming the
world? Do you here and now have the witness within
that you are His? Or are you in the sad plight of
those who are trying to live the new life with an old
heart?

Doubtless there are many here who are utter
strangers to this blessed experience. If so, let me insist
that it need not be the case. Now, in this service Christ
offers you the same privilege that He offered this man
years ago. You may be born again, now in a moment,
in the twinkling of an eye. "There is life for a look at
the Crucified One. There is life at this moment for
thee." Will you claim it? I know there are hindrances.
I know the enemy will suggest many difficulties. I
know cowardice will tug at you. But break away, as
did Nicodemus, and come even though you have to
come hounded by your fears. Christ waits to receive
you and to remake you. For this is His sure promise:
"Him that cometh unto me I will in no wise cast out."

V

THE SAINT'S SECRET—PAUL

Galatians 2:20

"I am crucified with Christ; nevertheless I live; yet
not I, but Christ liveth in me: and the life that I now
live in the flesh I live through faith in the Son of God,
who loved me, and gave himself for me." The Apostle
speaks of "the life that I now live." He is telling us
that he is not living today as he lived on a certain yesterday. A great change has been wrought. A wonderful transformation has taken place. The life that he
now lives is as far different from the life of other years
as light is different from darkness, as right is different
from wrong, as Heaven is different from hell.

What manner of life, then, is the apostle living now?
Answer: He is living the life of a saint. He has become a Christian. But what change has that wrought
in him? In other words, what is it to be a Christian?
The word is one of the most familiar in the language.
It is one that we use constantly. Yet I am persuaded
that there are many of us, even within the Church, who
have but a faint conception of the vast wealth of its
meaning. Being a Christian according to popular conception means, I fear, but very little. But being a
Christian according to the New Testament means
much. In fact, its meaning is deeper than the deepest
sea and higher than the heavens and wider than the
spaces between the stars.

But what, I repeat, had becoming a Christian done for Paul? It had not simply made him religious. He was religious before he ever passed through that marvelous experience on the road from Jerusalem to Damascus. You may be exceedingly religious and exceedingly unchristian at the same time. Neither did this experience end in simply giving Paul a new creed. It did that. Paul changed from an unbeliever to a believer in Christ. His views became orthodox. But a man may have very orthodox views about Christ and not be a Christian. The devil himself is entirely orthodox. He believes, the Word tells us, but that belief does not make him a saint. It only makes him shudder.

On what ground, then, did Paul base his claim to being a Christian? This is the answer: "Christ liveth in me." He is a Christian by virtue of the fact that he is indwelt by the personal, living, reigning Christ. And Paul did not look upon his experience as unique. He expected that same experience to be the lot of every Christian. His prayer for the saints at Ephesus was that Christ might dwell in their hearts rightly. He reminded the Corinthians that they were the temples of the living God. He told the church at Colosse that his mission was to declare to them "the riches of the glory of this mystery, Christ in you, the hope of glory." And he declares that anything less than Christ within would leave you less than a Christian. "If any man have not the Spirit of Christ, he is none of His."

"Christ liveth in me." No claim could be more wonderful. Is there any way of testing the truth of it? Suppose I were to say to you that the spirit of the artist Turner dwelleth in me. What manner of man would you expect me to be? You would expect me to have some of his fine discernment. You would expect me to see in the sunsets something of what he saw. You would expect this hand of mine to have something of the cunning of his hand. You would expect me to steal "the fleece from God's clouds and the sheen from God's rivers" and the lurid flash of God's lightning and fling them there upon the canvas. If I possessed only the eye of a bat and the skill of a ditch digger you would be slow to acknowledge my claim to possess the spirit of the great artist.

"Christ liveth in me," declares the apostle. Then we shall expect to see in the man making this amazing claim something of the beauty and power of Christ Himself. It is vain for any of us to say, "Christ liveth in me" and yet our lives be exactly as the lives of those who make no such claim. It would be vain for a world draped in midnight to boast of noonday splendors. I will tell you in vain of a fountain for the satisfying of the thirsts of men when my own tongue is swollen and my own lips are chapped and parched and dry.

Here is a man who says, "Christ liveth in me." If that is true we have a right to expect him to show forth something of the holiness of Christ. Christ said to his antagonists, "What man of you convinceth me of sin?" He claimed to live above sin. Not only so. He claimed to enable you and me to live above it. His name was to be called Jesus for the simple reason that He was to save His people from their sins. When John saw Him he pointed Him out as the Lamb of God who was to take away the sin of the world. He was to deliver men not only from the penalty of sin, but from its power as well.

Did Paul enter into this experience? The Record shows that he did. He confesses that there was a time when he was a bond slave to sin. He tells us of the terrible agony of his awful slavery. The good that he wanted to do he could not do and the evil that he hated he did. Sin wound itself about him like the coils of a serpent. In the bitterness of his despair we hear him cry: "O wretched man that I am, who shall deliver me?" And he found his answer in Jesus Christ. "I thank God, through Jesus Christ our Lord." "There is therefore now no condemnation to them which are in Christ Jesus. . . . The law of the Spirit of life has made us free."

This deliverance of Paul was not only a single experience, but it was his continued experience. So much was this the case that we find him saying to his fellow disciples, "Sin shall not have dominion over you." He even dared to write this brave word: "Reckon ye yourselves as dead indeed unto sin; but alive unto God through Jesus Christ."

Now Paul wrote constantly out of his own experience. This experience had led him to believe that there was a possibility of complete victory over all the powers of the enemy. "Reckon ye yourselves to be dead and count yourselves as free from sin and sinning as dead men." Now I do not come to you this morning to preach fanaticism. But I do come to tell you about your privileges as Christian people. And one of these privileges, if the New Testament is true, is living a life of victory over sin.

Where are we suffering more than we are suffering right here? Our lives are so mean and worldly that many of us have ceased to expect any power for conquest through Christ. We enter upon the Christian life without any expectation of victory. A girl said recently in speaking of her marriage that she did not know how she and Tom would hit it off, but they were going to try it out. If they didn't like it they could quit. What is to be expected of a marriage like that? Nothing but disaster. When good people marry they give themselves each to other. They absolutely foreclose their minds against any other love. I have absolutely no patience with the married man or woman that makes love to or accepts it from another. I do not believe it is ever innocent. If you are faithful to your marriage vows such a thing is an impossibility to you.

And, my brethren, we are a part of the bride of Christ. In giving ourselves to Him we are expected to close our minds and hearts against any other allegiance. And we are to count on victory through grace. If such a victory were an impossibility it would never have been promised. But it is promised over and over again. Hence it is to be claimed.

Of course, if we are left to win this victory in our own strength it is nothing short of madness to expect to triumph. But if it is true that Christ dwells within us, if we have an infinitely mighty Savior homing in our hearts, are such expectations mad or extravagant? The schoolhouse that I used to attend when a boy was surrounded by a forest of scrubby black oaks. When the frost came and loosened the grip of the leaves on other trees it seemed only to tighten the hold of these sear leaves upon the oaks. The ice and the snow and the winter winds were powerless to make these oak trees give up their burden of death. But by and by there was a new warmth in the atmosphere. There was a new note in the song of the bird. Spring came and slipped into the hearts of these oaks. It stole up through their branches. And then one day a new leaf said to the old dead leaf, "Make room, please." And life had come and death had gone. It had been brought about not by a power without, but by a power within. "Christ liveth in me." Therefore I have a right to expect triumph over all the power of the enemy.

"Christ liveth in me." Then we shall expect to find in this man Paul something of Christ's attitude toward the world. It will be worse than vain for him to make this claim and be selfish and listless and indifferent. Christ had a passion for men. He could not see a crowd without holding out His hands to them and saying, "Come to me." He could not pass a leper without putting the touch of His love upon him. A man who has this living Christ in his heart must be a lover.

And here, too, Paul makes good his claim. I hear him wishing that he might be accursed of God for his brethren, his kinsmen according to the flesh. Another time he is bearing the burdens of a runaway slave. "I beseech you for my son, whom I have begotten in my bonds, Onesimus by name. If he oweth thee anything, put that on my account. I, Paul, have written it with mine own hand, I will repay it." Another time it is no longer a slave, but a king. And yet there is that same note of yearning and passion: "I would God that not only thou, but all these that hear me this day, were both almost and altogether such as I am except these bonds." "Christ liveth in me," declares the Apostle. And when we get a glimpse into his heart we say, "Amen and Amen."

The Christ did not only love. But Christ did what love always does. He suffered. He gave himself sacrificially to the task of saving the world. What He did by a single act on Calvary was what He was doing every day of His life. His whole ministry was baptized with the spirit of sacrificial service.

"Christ liveth in me." Then my own life shall be

baptized in that same spirit. And such was the case with the great Apostle. "I fill up that which is behind of the sufferings of Christ in my body." Paul did not only serve. He served sacrificially. "Master, the Jews have sought to stone thee, and goest thou thither again?" And Jesus went back the path, Dr. Jowett tells us, that led to the stones. And we read of him in whom Christ lived: "They drew him out of the city and stoned him and left him for dead." But he, too, walked the path that led back to the stones. He was indwelt by the Christ who died. Therefore he himself declared that he "died daily."

We meet together this morning as Christians. As Christians we have a right to say, "Christ liveth in me." Do we say it in the love of Christ? Are we filling up, in any measure, that which is behind of the sufferings of Christ? Oh, how little of real sacrifice there is in the life of the ordinary member of the church of today. How few of us seek to please God rather than ourselves. In our church work many of us are worthless simply because we are unwilling to put ourselves to the trouble that it costs to be useful. Remember this, that if any man hath not the Spirit of Christ, which is the spirit of love, which is a spirit that makes us willing to bleed in order to bless, he is none of His.

"Christ liveth in me." Then we shall expect that this man's life shall be a fruitful life. We shall expect that where he farms the same kind of harvest shall grow that grows under the farming of Christ Himself. "He that believeth on me, the works that I do shall he do also. And greater works than these shall he do, because I go to my Father." And Paul's efforts did accomplish results. Lives were remade under his ministry and the world still feels the uplift of his mighty, Christ-filled personality.

"Christ liveth in me." How did Paul come to realize this? It was not by any magic. It was not by the works of the law. He reached it by an old and familiar road. "The life that I now live I live through faith in the Son of God, who loved me and gave himself for me." Christ had entered this life through faith. Christ had filled his life in response to faith.

And this, you see, was a personal faith. "Through faith in the Son of God who loved me and gave himself for me." Experiential religion, Luther tells us, is in the personal pronouns. It means very little for us to say, "Christ died for the world." We must come to where we can say, "He died for me." It is not enough to say, "Christ loved the world." We must be gripped by the blessed fact that "He loved me." It is not much to say, "The Lord is their shepherd." It is everything to say, "The Lord is my shepherd." "He loved me and gave Himself for me." Paul simply accepted Christ as the one infinitely mighty and infinitely willing to help. And clinging to Him by faith he lived the life of victory over sin and of marvelous service.

Now I wonder if it is not the longing of your heart that this experience of the Apostle be your experience. "Christ liveth in me." Has it been true? Is it true today? Do you not realize with myself that you have not enjoyed this experience in the richness and fullness that it is your privilege to enjoy it? Have you not been a bit of a disappointment to yourself and to your Lord?

It is said that an intimate friend of the great artist Millais went early one morning to an art gallery to see a display of his paintings. As she was going up the steps she saw the artist coming down. He tried to avoid her, but could not. When she came face to face with him she saw that his cheeks were wet with tears. "My lady," he said, "I am sorry that you have found me thus unmanned. I have just been looking at my early paintings. I find that they promised far more than I have ever attained. I have not realized my possibilities. That is what has broken my heart." Have you realized yours? If not, will you begin anew this morning? "Behold, I stand at the door and knock." As you gather round this table to take these symbols of the sacrificial death of our Lord, will you not by faith receive Him and count on Him to enter as He promises He will enter? Then you, too, will be able to say, "Christ liveth in me." Then you, too, will be able to show forth in the life you live the mighty power of the indwelling Christ.

VI

PERPETUAL THANKSGIVING—PAUL

I Thessalonians 5:18

"In everything give thanks." This exhortation sent by Paul to a group of his fellow Christians has a decided flavor of the impossible about it. The heights to which it calls seem far too rugged and steep for our feeble feet. So much is this the case that vast numbers of us never think of taking his great word seriously. We simply pass it by, confessing, of course, the reality of the pot of gold, but never forgetting that this gold is at the end of the rainbow, and is therefore quite beyond our reach.

But the Apostle himself was perfectly serious and genuinely sincere in the giving of this exhortation. He believed that it was possible to make every day a Thanksgiving Day. Nor did he hold this high conviction simply as a theory. It was his experience. As you study his life you find him in many a trying situation. At times you find him without his cloak, at times without his books and his parchments. You even find him without his freedom and without his friends. But never once do you find him without his song of thanksgiving.

"In everything give thanks." This is something more than a piece of good advice. Excellent advice it is, but it is far more. It is a command. It is a command that is binding. It brings in its hands the sanction of an infinite authority. "In everything give thanks."

So we see then that gratitude is not a matter that is purely optional. You cannot be a Christian and be grateful or ungrateful just as it suits you. To refuse to be thankful is to refuse to be obedient. And to refuse to be obedient is to refuse to be a Christian at all. So it is only stating a sober truth when we say that it is impossible for a thankless man to be a follower of Jesus Christ.

And you will notice the wide scope of this command. "In everything give thanks." That takes in a sweep so wide, I repeat, that it looks utterly impossible. In fact, it is impossible except we receive help from above. God is constantly calling upon us to do the impossible. It was impossible for the paralyzed man to rise and walk, but as he was willing Christ made the impossible to become the possible. And so God will do in this instance if we will allow Him.

"In everything give thanks." I wonder if we have ever been really serious and in earnest with this command. Notice what it says: "In everything." In the joy things and in the sorrow things, in the laughter-laden things and in the tearful things, in the things bright with morning and the things dark with night. "In everything give thanks."

Now that means that we are to be thankful when we succeed. That we are to be grateful in the moments of prosperity and of victory. It means also that we are to be thankful when we fail. That in the midst of our defeat and our humiliation our hearts are to still be overflowing with gratitude. We are to be thankful when these bodies of ours are athrill with vigor and life. We are also to be thankful when the destroying hand of disease is upon us and we feel ourselves slipping inch by inch into the grave.

"In everything." Truly it is a broad command. We are to be grateful when friends are kind, when they throw bouquets at us, when they grip our hands and tell us how much they appreciate us. We are to be thankful when friends seem unkind, when they throw mud at us instead of flowers, when they pass us by in forgetfulness and cold neglect. We are to be thankful beside the cradle afrolic with life. We are also to be thankful beside the grave gloomy with death.

This is indeed a high standard that our Lord sets for us through His inspired Apostle. But it is a possible standard. He never calls us to do that which through His grace we cannot do. How can we reach that fine mountain height where we will really be able to "In everything give thanks"? How did Paul reach it? He did not do so by getting into circumstances that were altogether favorable. Nor will we. There will never come a time in our lives when everything will come to us right-side up. We are going to have to pass through sorrows and losses, struggles and perplexities. However dry our cheeks are today, one day they are going to be wet with tears. So if we never expect to be thankful in everything until everything gets to be entirely to our liking, then we will never fulfill this command at all. But this gratitude is not a child of circumstances. The truth of the matter is that gratitude is never born purely of our circumstances.

For instance, the most grateful people are not the people who have the most. They are not the people who are blessed with good health and with sound minds and with beautiful homes and with high social circles. The most grateful people that I have met are often the

ones who, so far as the world could see, had the least.
Read the letters of Paul. He was always breaking out
into the gladdest praise. His letters are exultant with
thanksgiving. They ring with triumphant hallelujahs.
This is true not because Paul had everything. He was
being shipwrecked, stoned, hounded, whipped, im-
prisoned. At last they killed him, but they never killed
his gratitude.

How then, I repeat, is this amazing possibility to
be realized? Answer, it is to be realized through faith
in God. Gratitude is a child of faith. If you ever get
to the place where you can really give thanks in everything, you have got to have a very real and very vital
grip of God. You have got to believe that Paul speaks
the sober truth when he says, "All things work together
for good to them that love God." There will be many
times, of course, when you do not see how the trials and
defeats that come upon you can be for good. There
will be many times when you cannot understand. But
remember that it is not necessary to understand. It is
only necessary to believe.

When Bunyan was shut up in Bedford jail he could
not understand just how this could be best. But God
wanted him to preach, not simply to the men of his day,
but to the men of all time. And so He locked in Bunyan's body that his soul might be out piloting the pil-
grims over the eventful road from the City of Destruction to Mt. Zion. Believe me, the rude block of marble
must have great faith in the art and in the skill of the
sculptor if it is to be grateful while it is undergoing the
disturbing strokes of mallet and chisel. But if it can
be brought to believe that the sculptor is working toward
the liberation of the angel that is pent up within, it can,
even for these wounding strokes, give thanks.

Our unbelieving eyes looked out the other day and saw only the black clouds and the pouring rain, the soggy streets and the muddy roads and the water-soaked fields. Faith looked out and thanked God and sang:

"It isn't raining rain to me,
　It's raining daffodils;
In every dimpled drop I see
　Wild flowers upon the hills.

"A cloud of gray engulfs the day
　And overwhelms the town;
It isn't raining rain to me,
　It's raining roses down.

"It isn't raining rain to me,
　It's raining clover bloom,
Where any buccaneering bee
　Can find a bed and room.

"So a health to him who's happy,
　And a fig to him who frets;
It isn't raining rain to me,
　It's raining violets."

But while gratitude is a child of faith it is also a child that we must watch and train and develop. Gratitude, as all other fine graces, must be cultivated. It must be tended and watered and watched over or it will die. "In everything give thanks." Do not think that Paul reached this fine height without a struggle. Do not expect to do so yourself. You are not going to do that easily. You are not going to do it lazily and half asleep. You will never realize that high achievement except by conscious effort.

Now how can we help ourselves in the cultivation of

this rare and winsome flower called gratitude? In the first place, if you are going to be thankful in everything you cannot begin to do that by ignoring the daily blessings of life which we are accustomed to call commonplace. And yet that is just what most of us have a great tendency to do.

Some time ago I chanced to meet an old friend who had been a great sufferer from a most dreaded disease. But he was then recovered and in perfect health. His dreary days of depression and long nights of wretchedness had passed. And how happy he was. His very presence refreshed like sea breezes. He was simply bubbling over with gladsome praise and thanksgiving. But when I told an excellent woman about this meeting and the great gratitude of our friend what think you she said? This: "Of course! I would be thankful, too, if I had recovered from that terrible disease." Yet she seemed to forget to thank God that she had never even been sick at all.

Did you ever hear of that morning when the sun did not rise? One day—but it was not day. Six o'clock came and no roses bloomed in that far garden of the East. Seven o'clock came and still no sun and no ray of light. Then eight, then nine, then ten, then noon and at noon it was as black as midnight. At noon no bird sang. There was only the hoot of the owl and the swoop of the bat. The world lay dark and silent and asleep.

Then came the black hours of the black afternoon. And there was no sunset because there was no sunrise. And there was no retiring to bed where the weary sleep the "sleep that knits up the raveled sleave of care." Instead people remained wide awake. Some wept, some wrung their hands in anguish. Every church was

thronged to its doors with people upon their knees.
Thus they remained the whole night through and then
millions of eager and tear-wet faces were turned toward
the east. And when the sky began to grow red and the
sun looked up once more, there went up a shout of
great joy that was fairly echoed from star to star.
Now a hundred million lips said, "Bless the Lord, O
my soul."

Why were these people so thankful? It is the strang-
est reason in the world. They were thankful because
the sun failed to rise for one whole day. And thus the
very constancy of God's blessings sometimes seems to
kill our gratitude. We are so like little children. Take
your child a toy every day when you go home and it will
not be two weeks before he will cease to appreciate it,
will even feel himself wronged if it fails in a single
instance to come.

Cultivate then the fine habit of being thankful for
life's daily blessings. Appreciate God's mercies that
are new every morning. Commonplace as they seem
they are the blessings without which life would not be
worth the living. Appreciate the sunrises and the sunsets, the springtimes and the autumntides, the comforts
of home, the handclasp of friends, the confidence of
associates, the clinging love of the inner circle. Appreciate the open Bible, the Church with its welcome, the
constant invitation to the place of prayer and the wide
open gateway into the Father's house.

"In everything give thanks." If we do this we must,
in the second place, fling away our pride and self-
sufficiency and conceit. Did you ever notice how prone
we are to blame others for our misfortune and to thank
ourselves for our good fortune? The Rich Fool made
a fine crop, but he congratulated nobody but himself.

He thanked only his own prudence and keenness and sagacity.

How different was Paul. Having returned from a successful missionary journey he does not relate what he has done, but what God has done through him. Preaching before Agrippa and the great crowd in Cæsarea he does not boast of the wisdom that has enabled him to live in spite of bitter enemies. But he says: "Having therefore obtained help of God I continue unto this day." When accounting for himself this alone is his claim: "By the grace of God I am what I am."

May the Lord teach us a like wisdom. For what have I, what have you that we have not received? Have you ability in any direction? Are you physically attractive? Have you beauty? It is no mean gift. Have you strength of mind and of body? Have you a task, a place to work and skill to fill your place? If so, appreciate it. Remember that you have not simply yourself to thank for it. The truth of the matter is that there is not a single blessing that you possess today for which you have only yourself to thank.

If you have a tendency to self-conceit, ask yourself how much would be left if God took from you everything except what is due to yourself alone. If He should do so, civilization would be gone. You did not make it. This city would vanish. You did not build it. The sun would suddenly go out in the sky; the stars would vanish; this solid earth would drop like an anchor into the sea; the sea would vanish; your body would melt into thin air and your immortal soul would be annihilated. So if there is a single thing you value this morning give thanks for it because it comes to you as a gift.

Then if you are going to be grateful in everything you must, in the third place, refuse to allow the blessings of others to make you despise your own. It is strange that we should be so foolish and so wicked as to do this and yet we often are. Saul appreciated the praise that was given to him till he found that David had greater praise. You appreciated the little daisy that was put into your hand till you saw that a friend of yours had an American Beauty rose. You enjoyed your Ford till your friend began to ride in a Packard. Oh, you will never be grateful in that way.

Now, if you are obliged to contrast, contrast yourself as you are today with what you might have been but for the good and tender mercy of your Lord. Do you remember the demoniac that Jesus healed? He wanted to go with the Master, you remember, but Jesus sent him home. Do you suppose this man thought of John leaning upon the bosom of Jesus and plucked up the flower of gratitude and planted the nettle of envy in its place? No, I rather think that when he was so tempted he thought of the tombs in which he used to live and of the fetters with which men used to try to bind him and of the demons that once possessed him. And thinking of these things the nightingales of gratitude began to sing in the garden of his heart.

Last of all, if you are going to be thankful in everything you must cultivate the habit of giving expression to your thanks. That is what Paul did. He was forever telling his Lord and telling his friends how thankful he was. Constantly he was giving expression to his gratitude. And the more he gave expression to it the more thankful he became. For we are rich in the fine wealth of gratitude just in proportion as we give it away.

Of course those of us who never praise have a good excuse for our silence. Here it is:—God knows or our friends know that we are grateful. But that is not enough. God desires that we "give thanks." And we in this particular are like our Lord. How many starved hearts there are in the world because we fail to give expression to our gratitude. And how many of us allow our gratitude to become weak and sickly and often utterly dead because we fail to give expression to it.

One time a most wonderful preacher visited a certain village. In that village there were ten men who were dying of a hideous and loathsome disease. These wretched men formed themselves into a committee and asked this preacher for help. And the heart of the preacher was tender and his power great. So he responded to this committee of rottenness by healing them every one. This done, nine of them said: "He knows how grateful I am." And having so said they hurried away and ceased to be grateful at all. The tenth man came and fell down at his Savior's feet, giving Him thanks. And when he arose he had tenfold more gratitude than he had when he came. Therefore I urge, "Let the redeemed of the Lord say so."

Now what is the good of being grateful? "In everything give thanks." Why? The Apostle gives just one big reason. "This is the will of God." That is reason enough, is it not? He said be thankful in everything because God wants you to be. That is the way and the only way to please Him.

Why does our gratitude please God? First, because it is a mark of Christian growth in ourselves. Gratitude is a test of character. No baby is grateful. You can take your little fellow when he has the colic and walk the floor with him for seven long hours, and then when you put him down he will never say "Much obliged." He will just yell a little louder. Now we do not blame him, simply because he is a baby. But to continue to be ungrateful is to always be an infant. If you have no gratitude in your heart this morning that shows in itself that you are a moral dwarf. You may have the body of a giant and the mentality of a Shakespeare but you have the soul of a pigmy.

To be a thankful Christian is pleasing to God, in the next place, because to be grateful is one of the roadways to usefulness. Gratitude makes you helpful. It makes you helpful because it begets gratitude in others. Did you ever turn away from seeing some sick body who had neither health nor money nor social position and yet was full of gratitude? And you said to yourself: "Just look what I have. How thankful I ought to be." And you were helped toward gratitude by the gratitude of another.

Then we are helpful in other ways. How a little gratitude strengthens us sometimes. How much better we work when we know we are appreciated. Oh, I fancy that all the machinery of this world would run with infinitely greater smoothness if we would just oil it now and then with the fine oil of appreciation. We think lovely things. We say lovely things when folks are dead. But the trouble is we so often keep them secret while they are alive.

One day you look over the way and see crêpe on the door of your friend. You hurry over to where he lies asleep and spill a thousand grateful words into an ear that does not hear and into a heart that is not helped. But how much you might have helped if you had been in time. That was the fine thing about Mary. She gave expression to her appreciation and she did it on

time. "She came aforetime," said the Master. That
is, Mary with love's intuition saw Death coming in the
distance, and she said, "I will beat Death to Him."
And she did. So when Death touched His forehead it
made even his old frozen fingers smell of perfume.
This because Mary had been on time in giving expression to her gratitude.

> "If I should die tonight,
> My friends would look upon my quiet face
> Before they laid it in its resting-place,
> And deem that death had left it almost fair,
> And laying snow-white flowers upon my hair,
> Would smooth it down with lingering caress—
> Poor hands, so empty and so cold tonight!
>
> "If I should die tonight,
> My friends would call to mind, with loving thought,
> Some kindly deed the icy hand had wrought,
> Some gentle word the frozen lips had said—
> Errands on which the willing feet had sped;
> The memory of my selfishness and pride,
> My hasty words, would all be put aside,
> And so I should be loved and mourned tonight.
>
> "O friends, I pray tonight,
> Keep not your kisses for my dead cold brow.
> The way is lonely; let me feel them now.
> Think gently of me; I am travel-worn,
> My faltering feet are pierced with many a thorn.
> Forgive! O hearts estranged, forgive, I plead!
> When ceaseless bliss is mine I shall not need
> The tenderness for which I long tonight."

Then gratitude is pleasing to God because God is a
lover and love always wants to be appreciated. Understand, love will live without it, but it lives in grief and
pain and disappointment. If you love anybody the

keenest wound that they can inflict upon you is the wound of ingratitude. The high-water mark of English tragedy is King Lear. And what is the climax of this tragedy? It is the father learning "how sharper than a serpent's tooth it is to have a thankless child."

Did you ever read of how those that feared the Lord spoke about it and how a book of remembrance was kept? I wonder if the recording angel will be able to write your name and mine this morning in the gilded volume of those who are thankful. Believe me, you can bring no greater joy to your Lord than the fulfilling of this command: "In everything give thanks."

VII

THE FIELD PREACHER—THE LILY

Matthew 6: 28-29

"Consider the lilies of the field, how they grow; they toil not, neither do they spin: and yet I say unto you, that even Solomon in all his glory was not arrayed like one of these." Today, with the Master as our interpreter, we are going to attend church in the open fields. We are going away from the feverish and restless life of the city out into that great temple of the out-of-doors. We are going to that church whose dome is the sky, and whose carpet is the green earth, and whose walls are the far-flung horizons, and whose music is the sighing of the wind mingled with the song of the birds. And there we are going to listen reverently and attentively and hopefully, I trust, to a winsome field preacher whose name is The Lily.

As we enter this magnificent church in the open we are at once impressed by the personality of the preacher. "How attractive," we say to ourselves. "How wonderfully magnetic." In spite of our natural listlessness and spiritual stupidity we become eager and attentive. We find ourselves tingling with a delightful thrill of expectancy.

What is the secret of the compelling loveliness of this preacher? The Master, who above all others has the seeing eye and the understanding heart, is lavish in His praise: "Verily I say unto you that even Solomon in all his glory was not arrayed like one of these."

Of course there are many of us too blind to agree with Him. If we saw a lily and Solomon standing together we would doubtless give all our attention to Solomon. That is true from the simple fact that so many of us are more interested in the counterfeit than in the genuine. We like tinsel better than we do real gold. We thrill more over glass beads than we do over diamonds. We prefer the glow worm to the star.

What then, I repeat, is the glory of the lily? It is not in its richness of adornment. It is not in the wealth of what it has in its pocket. A man of great wealth and of little character said indignantly, "I'll have you to understand that I am worth a million pounds." "Yes," was the reply, "but not a cent more." That is, you are worth only the money that you possess. In yourself you are worth nothing. All your wealth is external to you. Yours is not the wealth of the glory of the lily.

Its glory did not consist, in the second place, in its rank. The Master did not call attention to the beauty of the flower pot in which the lily grew. He did not bid us consider what a skilled piece of work the flower pot was, how showily it was gilded. He did not call attention to the lily because it bloomed in the temple or on the steps of the throne. Its glory was not a glory of rank. It was not a glory of position. That is the only glory that some people ever get. Apart from the glory of the rank to which they were born they have no glory at all.

Its glory did not consist of its social position. Our attention is not directed to the lily because of its aristocratic neighbors. It may have had the most select social circle. It may have had a Marechal Neil and an American Beauty as its next-door neighbors, or it may have rubbed elbows on one side with the sour dock and on the other side with a rag weed. Nettles and night-shade may have flourished in the same block. But its glory was not a glory of its social position. The glory that it possessed was inherent in itself.

What was this glory? First of all, it was the glory of naturalness. When you stood in the presence of this lily preacher you were impressed with its sincerity, its utter freedom from affectation and cant. You could not believe that it was simply putting on a lily face to hide a dog fennel heart. You could not believe that thorns were hidden behind its velvet. You were impressed at once that it was just what it seemed to be and no more.

What a fine virtue is genuineness, frankness, open-hearted sincerity! How repellent is counterfeit, hypocrisy, insincerity! What poor creatures we become when we try to pose as other than we are and to impress people as being what we are not. There is something so restful and helpful and genuinely charming about one whom you can know to be transparently sincere and true.

The second glory of the lily is the glory of unspottedness. You could not get into its presence without being impressed and arrested and even made heart hungry by its purity. And while the word "good" has fallen upon evil days, while from misuse it is thoroughly decrepit and lame upon its feet—still this remains true, that genuine goodness, thorough unspottedness is the most winsome virtue that this world knows.

It is said that the mission workers in the East End of London used to always carry a white flower. And one night when one of these mission workers was sitting talking to an outcast woman to the surprise of the worker the woman suddenly began to weep. And when the missionary sought to know the reason, the outcast touched the petals of the flower with a faded finger and said, "I am not like that. I used to be like that." Against the white unspottedness of the flower she saw her own soiled and dirty life.

The lily is unspotted. What a virtue is that in the teacher. What a supreme requirement in the preacher! It is the one requirement without which he can never be at his best. He may fail in culture. He may fail in eloquence. He may fail in a thousand ways, but if he succeeds in this he will not be without a hearing and men will be helped as they hear him.

And let us not forget that the same God who gives spotlessness to the lily can and will give it to you and me. He is able and there is no other who is able. This word comes from the Divine lips and from no other lips: "Though your sins be as scarlet they shall be as white as snow." Bud Robinson tells us this bit of his hospital experience. He was in most intense pain. He had the nurse 'phone certain saintly friends to pray for him. Ease came at once and he went to sleep. While asleep he dreamed that he was in Heaven. One came to lead him into the presence of Christ. In that presence he had a vision of his own heart. He said, "It was a white heart. It was whiter than snow." And this, thank God, is the high privilege that He offers to every one of us.

So you see we have in this field preacher the very graces that we most need and most desire for ourselves. Is it not fine when you can believe that the man who preaches to you and teaches you, that the man who is trying to lead you really knows that of which he speaks? Would it not be great if every preacher could

say, as did Saint Paul, "Follow me as I follow Christ"?
How splendid it would be if we could always say, "All
these graces of which I am speaking to you are actual
experiences in my own life!"

Inasmuch then as this lily has arrived, we would like
to know how it arrived. Suppose the preacher tells his
experience. And we look down into the face of this
lovely flower and say, "You are sincere. You are
guileless. You are unspotted. You are winsome and
fragrant. How did you come to be what you are? Is
there not magic in it? Were you touched by some
wonderful wand and made suddenly into what you
are?"

And what says the lily? It shakes its lovely head:
"Ah, no; there is no magic in it. I grew. 'Consider
the lilies how they grow.'" Then we say in surprise,
"There was a time when you were not as beautiful as
you are today?" "Ah, yes," comes the ready answer.
"I was once only a little bulb. And then there was a
time when I was even more insignificant than that. I
have arrived to where I am today not all at once, but
little by little.

"And there is another fact you must not forget,"
says the lily. "And that is that while I grew I did
not do so independently. The words of Paul are tremendously true for me, 'For to me to live is Christ.'
Back of my birth is God. It was through Him that
I began to live. It is through Him that I have continued to live. He is the source of all my beauty. You
see this garment that I wear. Human fingers never
wove one so beautiful. It was woven by His hands.
It is from Him that all my growth has come. It is in
His soil that I rooted myself and it is His sun that
has warmed me and lighted my way."

And what the lily is trying to tell us is that we too may grow. When we study the lives of the conspicuous saints we see that they did not attain all at once. They grew. The Apostle John—what does his name suggest to you? It suggests love. It is the name that has come to have a tender caress in it, and yet John was not always an apostle of love. Who is that man there interfering with the religious work of his brother? "We saw one casting out devils in thy name and we forbade him because he followed not us." Who said that? John said it—John, the beloved Apostle.

Here is another scene. Jesus is on His way to Jerusalem. He seeks to spend the night at a little Samaritan village. But the people are ignorant and full of prejudice. They are blind to their opportunity. They refuse their hospitality to the Master and His disciples. Some of the company do not take the refusal with Christian sweetness. "Shall we command fire to come down from Heaven and destroy them?" asked one. Who wanted to burn these poor misguided and ignorant folks? That man was John, John who afterward became the Apostle of Love and whose very message to the world can almost be summed up in this sentence: "Brethren, love one another." The secret of John is that he grew.

Now, that is the secret of this lily preacher. And as we see its winsomeness we too would like to grow. So as we lean forward toward this fascinating preacher this is what our hearts are saying: "I wonder how you managed to grow. I wonder how it came to pass that you won that 'fulfilling sense of glad obedience that made thee all that nature meant thee.' Did you get restless and worried and anxious? Did you fret yourself into growth and beauty?"

"No," answered the lily. "I did not grow by worrying about it. I have not attained the height to which
I have attained through anxiety." The secret of the
lily is its restfulness, its utter freedom from worry. It
did not attain perfection by fretting itself into a fever.
And you will not and I will not. This lily preaches
a wonderfully convincing sermon against our care-filled
and harassed and troubled lives. It tells us that we
will never find peace, that we will never find victory,
that we will never really grow till we trust God enough
to stop our fretting and our worrying.

Neither did the lily grow by squaring its jaw and
making a great determination to grow. Had it said
one day, "Go to now, I am going to do some growing,"
and then had measured itself every morning and every
night and kept its finger on its pulse, I doubt if it
would have ever grown. There is a law known as the
law of indirection which means that the best way to
attain is the indirect way. For instance, the best way
to go to sleep is to forget all about trying to go to
sleep. The harder you try the wider awake you become. The best way to be happy is not to work yourself into a fever trying to amuse yourself. It is to forget your own happiness in an effort to bring happiness
to others. And the best way to grow is not to quit
everything else and give yourself up to an attempt to
grow.

How did this lily grow? First, it grew by being
submissive to the Divine will. Had you sat down beside
this lily and talked to it it might have said to you
after this fashion: "There was once a time when I
rebelled at the very thought of being a lily. I wanted
to be a sunflower. Then I saw that big oak standing
yonder and thought how much longer it would last than

I would last and I wanted to be an oak. It cut me to the heart that I would only live for one short season. But by and by I came to realize that if God had wanted me for an oak He would have made me one. I realized that the best and wisest thing for me was to be in glad submission what God intended me to be.

"But even after this my fight was not over. One day when I had made up my mind to be a lily and be content with the lot of lilyhood, just then something else happened that disturbed me greatly. Somebody came and dug up my neighbor and I learned that he placed it in a lovely pot and carried it into a church. And then I wondered why I had to stay here in this lonely spot. I knew of some lilies that bloomed in the royal gardens where hundreds saw them every day. And when I read, 'Full many a flower is born to blush unseen and waste its sweetness on the desert air,' I rebelled and grew restless and wretched because that seemed to be my lot. But I have learned better now," said the lily with glad face, "and I am happy to be what I am and where I am."

And now I wonder if you have become thus wise? There was a time, possibly, when you were much dissatisfied that you were yourself. And you wondered why you could not have been another with another's opportunity and another's ability. And there was a time when your lot vexed you and almost broke your heart and you did not understand why it was that while others were given the privilege of serving in some conspicuous way, your lot seemed to be to suffer in obscurity and in silence. Your eyes were bent upon far horizons, but the hand of Providence held you back. You wanted to go into the big world beyond the hills and you have been forced to stay where you are.

I wonder if you have learned that God's way is best.
I wonder if having learned to sing, "I'll go where you
want me to go," you have also learned this finer song:

"I'll stay where you've put me, I will, dear Lord,
   Though I wanted so badly to go.
I was eager to march at the battle front,
   I wanted to lead them, you know.
I planned to keep step to the music loud,
   To cheer when the banner unfurled,
To stand in the midst of the fight straight and proud,
   When the enemy's darts were hurled—
But I'll stay where you've put me.

"I'll stay where you've put me, I will, dear Lord,
   Though the field be narrow and small,
And the ground lies fallow and the stones are thick
   And there seems to be no life at all.
The field is thine own—only give me the seed,
   And I'll sow it with never a fear;
I'll till the dry soil while I wait for the rain
   And rejoice when the green blades appear.
I'll stay where you've put me.

"I'll stay where you've put me, I'll work, dear Lord,
   I'll bear the day's burden and heat,
Always trusting thee fully. When evening is come
   I'll lay heavy sheaves at thy feet.
And then when my life work is ended and done,
   In the light of eternity's glow—
Life's record all closed I surely shall find
   'Twas better to stay than to go—
So I'll stay where you've put me."

"A second lesson I learned," said the lily, "was the
lesson of appropriation. I waited a long time for
something wonderful, something out of the ordinary to
happen. I thought maybe an angel might come one
day with a golden pitcher to give me a drink. I thought

one day some marvelous new light might appear in the sky to give me warmth and brightness. But I have ceased to either expect or desire these. I have learned simply to take what God gives day by day and night by night. And you know since I have learned that I have never wanted.

"Every night, you see, I drink from the mystic chalice of the dew. Every morning the sun bursts with new glad radiance upon me. Also in proportion as I have need I receive the gentle baptism of the rain. Meantime rare nuggets of beauty are placed in my hands by the rich loam of the garden. And I have learned from my own experience that my God shall 'supply all my needs according to His riches in glory.'"

And do we not need amidst the fitful fever of our lives to learn this lesson of appropriation? How much God longs to give us and how little we are willing to take! He wants to make us rich and we insist on remaining miserably poor. He wants to make us kings and we insist on remaining slaves. Oh, that we might learn from the lily's lips that "He that spared not His own Son, but freely offered Him up for us all will also with Him freely give us all things"!

"Then I have one other blessed secret that God has taught me," said the lily. "When I first began to grow I was very happy. Then the bees began to buzz about me and now and then the humming birds would come and the toilers in the field would look upon me and the winds would seem to be trying to steal all my perfume. And I became afraid I would have nothing left. I tried to veil my face and shut my hands so as to hold the wealth that God had given me. But I had no sooner begun that than I discovered that I was withering. Today"—and the lily laughed outright—"I offer myself to all comers. Every bird and bee is welcomed and I try to look as sweet and fresh and spotless for a beggar as I would for a king. I have learned that the fine art of living is the art of giving."

And if there is a most important truth in the sermon of the lily I suppose this is it. One reason we have not grown is because we have been unwilling to serve, unwilling to give. Remember that it is literally true, that "he that saveth his life shall lose it." If God has blessed you with ability, use it. If God has blessed you with opportunity, use it. If God has blessed you with a vision of His face, tell that vision for His glory. If God has put money in your hands dedicate it to Him. Submit yourself to His will. Open your heart to receive what He longs to give you. Open your hands to pass on to others what He longs to give them. And you will approach more and more to the winsome beauty of the lily.

And then this last word. And the preacher is speaking solemnly and yet with a brave and submissive cheer. And this is the message: "God has done all this for me though I am to live but for one day. 'Today I am and tomorrow I am cast into the oven. Will He not much more do this for you, O ye of little faith?' You are to live forever. You are to live when the stars have fallen like unripe figs and when 'this world has dropped like an anchor in the sea.' Depend upon it, therefore, that the God who gives such surpassing beauty to the lily that blooms for a day, will give a yet surer and greater beauty to you human flowers that bloom through all eternity." Therefore, "Consider the lilies how they grow; they toil not neither do they spin: and yet I say unto you that even Solomon in all his glory was not arrayed like one of these."

VIII

SCARECROWS—THE MAN OF ONE TALENT

Matthew 25: 14-30

My subject is not original. It was suggested by that delightful essayist, Frank Boreham. In the course of a walk one day, he tells us, he came upon a lovely garden. In the center of this garden was a strikingly ugly scarecrow. Its weather-beaten garments hung about it in horrid awkwardness. Its worn-out hat was tilted at that ungainly angle that denotes disgraceful drunkenness. Its ghastly arms were outstretched as if to gather to its embrace any luckless individual who would dare to trespass upon the premises it had been set to guard.

But what filled this essayist with wonder and delight was this: a blackbird was sitting upon each one of the outstretched arms of this appalling scarecrow. These fortunate birds were looking complacently and triumphantly down at the strawberries that were ripening at their feet. They had already had a very wholesome banquet, and they would enjoy another as soon as their hunger demanded it. I am not sure that he tipped his hat to these wise birds, but in his heart he gave them great applause.

But all the birds that he saw in his walk were not in the strawberry patch. There were some perched upon the fence posts. Others were upon telegraph poles. Others chirped disconsolately from tree-tops. All of them seemed to look hungrily and longingly at the juicy berries that were ripening about the feet of the scarecrow. There was the most delightful food within their reach, but they were not getting a single berry. The reason they were not doing so was because they were frightened away by the terrible effigy that stood guard in the center of the garden.

Now when I read that story my memory literally began to swarm with scarecrow stories. They came to me out of my own experience and out of the experience of others. I thought of them in literature. I thought of the ones I had read in the Word of God. Some wise man could compile a small library made up exclusively of scarecrow stories.

But the best scarecrow story I know is one that fell from the Master's lips. We read it in the twenty-fifth chapter of St. Matthew. "For the kingdom of Heaven is as a man traveling into a far country, who called his own servants, and delivered unto them his goods. And unto one he gave five talents, to another two, and to another one; to every man according to his several ability; and straightway took his journey. Then he that had received the five talents went and traded with the same, and made them other five talents. And likewise he that had received two, he also gained other two. But he that had received one went and digged in the earth, and hid his lord's money.

"After a long time the lord of those servants cometh, and reckoneth with them. And so he that had received five talents came and brought other five talents, saying, Lord, thou deliveredst unto me five talents: behold I have gained beside them five talents more. His lord said unto him, Well done, good and faithful servant; thou hast been faithful over a few things, I will make thee ruler over many things; enter thou into the joy of thy lord. He also that had received two talents came and said, Lord, thou deliveredst unto me two talents: behold, I have gained two other talents beside them. His lord said unto him, Well done, good and faithful servant; thou hast been faithful over a few things, I will make thee ruler over many things: enter thou into the joy of thy lord.

"Then he which had received the one talent came and said, Lord, I knew thee that thou art a hard man, reaping where thou hast not sown, and gathering where thou hast not strewed. And I was afraid, and went and hid thy talent in the earth: lo, there thou hast that is thine. His lord answered and said unto him, Thou wicked and slothful servant, thou knewest that I reap where I sowed not, and gathered where I have not strewed. Thou oughtest therefore to have put my money to the exchanges, and then at my coming I should have received mine own with usury. Take therefore the talent from him, and give it unto him which hath ten talents. For unto every one that hath shall be given, and he shall have abundance; but from him that hath not shall be taken away even that which he hath. And cast ye the unprofitable servant into outer darkness: there shall be weeping and gnashing of teeth."

There are three characters in this story. Two of them thrill us with delight and admiration. It is an inspiration to see their strong purposefulness. We love to watch their strenuous and intelligent endeavor. Above all else we are delighted to see them come forward on the day of reckoning each having doubled his original store. Our hearts sing with their hearts as we hear the words of their master: "Well done, good and faithful servant: thou hast been faithful over a few things, I will make thee ruler over many things: enter thou into the joy of thy lord."

But the third man fills us with pain and shame and pity. He makes no effort. He wins no prize. He is greeted with no commendation from his master. Instead, his talent is taken from him. He is bound hand and foot and flung out into the dark. Not in all the wide world could you find a more pathetic failure than he.

Why the difference between these men? Why the difference between the birds of which we spoke? While these two brave blackbirds are eating the choice berries of the garden, I question with a third that is looking at them hungrily from a safe perch on the bough of a neighboring tree. "Have you had any berries this morning?" "No," he replies with a whine that almost has a sob in it. "Why is that?" I ask. "Were they all parched by the drouth or killed by the frost?" "No," he answers. "There are enough berries over yonder fifty feet away to last me a lifetime." Then I reply, "Why in the name of all that is reasonable do you not go to dinner?" And he points to the scarecrow and says: "There! I am afraid of that." And then I say: "What a foolish bird you are."

But why call this bird foolish? For the simple reason that he will allow himself to be robbed of the prizes he most covets by a harmless scarecrow. He permits himself to be cheated by such groundless fears. He sits and starves, not because there is nothing to eat, but because he is too cowardly to claim his privileges. And of the same type was the man of one talent. He failed not because he had no chance. He failed not for lack of ability. He failed because he was afraid. "I was afraid." He was defeated by a few scarecrows.

What were some of the scarecrows that robbed this poor fellow? First there was the scarecrow of his own seeming littleness. He was very proud of his talent till he met a man one day who had two talents. Then later he met another man who had five. Then he said: "These men are far more capable than I. They have so much more ability. If I had ten talents I would do big things myself, but as I have only one there is no use for me to try."

What a common scarecrow this is. How many of us have been frightened into utter uselessness by the thought of our own insignificance. We say if we could sing as well as John McCormack, or if we could preach as well as Paul, if we had as much money as Henry Ford we would turn the world upside down. But inasmuch as we are what we are and inasmuch as we have what we have, we will do nothing at all. That is exactly the same scarecrow that kept the ten spies out of the Land of Promise. They told themselves that they did not count. "We were in our own eyes as grasshoppers."

Now I am not urging you to any sense of self-importance or conceit. I am not encouraging you to believe as did the old-time cock that the sun rises every morning to hear you crow. A few people fail from over-estimating themselves, but far more fail from thinking too meanly of themselves. Besides, you are not to be judged according to your accomplishment. You are to be judged according to your faithfulness. You are not going to be questioned as to what you would have done with ten talents. You are going to be questioned upon what you actually did with one. Do not let the scarecrow of your own smallness cheat you of the highest possible success—that of being faithful.

A second scarecrow that this man saw in the garden was that of unfavorable circumstances. He said, "If I were living anywhere else except where I am, I could easily make my one talent into two. If I had some other market in which to do business, if I were living in yesterday or in tomorrow instead of this prosaic today, I could do something. But since I am living as I am and where I am, there is no chance." So the strawberries rotted and he never tasted a one of them.

And here are you tonight. You have heard the Gospel since your earliest recollections. You have always expected to be a Christian some time. It is your ambition in a hazy sort of way to serve. But the time that you are going to do that is tomorrow. And the place you are going to do that is anywhere except here. This church is so big, it is so crowded, it is so full of strangers it doesn't need you. You will wait, therefore, and fling away your today in the vain hope that in some other time and in some other place you will find a life of Christian service altogether easy. Thus you are frightened into uselessness by the scarecrow of circumstances.

The third scarecrow that kept this man out of the garden was a mistrust of his lord. Listen to what he thinks of him: "I knew that thou art a hard man, taking up that thou layest not down and gathering where thou hast not sowed." In other words his master is not fair. He is not just. He is not going to give him a square deal.

Now this man is not in a class by himself. There are not a few who feel just that way about Jesus Christ.

We may not be bold enough to say so. We may not think quite clearly enough to state it in plain words as this man did. Yet the fact remains that we mistrust the fairness and the justice of our Lord. We hear His promises and refuse to accept them as true. "Him that cometh unto me I will in no wise cast out," He says. And yet we doubt the fact that He will receive ourselves.

Or we have a fear that He has set for us a task that we cannot accomplish. It has never occurred to us to deny the beauty of Christlike character. We have profound admiration for a genuine Christian. We flatter ourselves that we would very much delight in being true saints of God. But the task is quite too high. It is beyond our feeble strength. But if this is true, whose fault is it then that we are not Christians? It is not our own, but God's. Therefore, if we are condemned for our failure we have not had a square deal. God is for us a hard master. He is not just.

What a hideous scarecrow is this. How dangerous and how damning. There is no greater dishonor that we can do our Lord than to mistrust Him. Shall not the Judge of all the earth do right? He shall. He does. There is not a promise that He is not eager to keep with you. There is no spiritual treasure that He is not willing to put into your hands. Dare to fling yourself upon His mercy and you will find that He will not fail you. What greater calamity can come to any man than the calamity of suspecting, of mistrusting God? Such a man slams every door in his own face. Believe it, God's commands to you are capable of being carried out. He is infinitely just and fair. If you will test Him you will find Him true.

The fourth scarecrow that frightened this poor fellow

was the possibility of failure. He was afraid to fail. "Have you had any berries?" I ask one of these hungry birds perched outside the garden. And he answers, "No." "Why not? Are there not berries just inside the palings yonder?" "Yes," he answers sadly, "but I am afraid if I go I will not get any, or I am afraid if I did get a berry something would make me drop it before I could ever get out." Foolish bird. And far more foolish men. Before you learned to box or to play tennis or to do anything else you had to risk failing at it. Not only so, but you failed at it at the beginning. To be so afraid of failing as to refuse to try is to make the supreme failure. What greater calamity is there than to be so afraid that you will fall that you never dare to stand on your feet.

Tonight I invite you to become an earnest and active Christian. Not only so, but through me Jesus Christ is inviting you. But you say, "I am afraid I could never hold out." But could there be any greater failure than to refuse to try? When did it ever come to pass that an honest effort made matters worse? Suppose you were to make a sincere and earnest endeavor to be a Christian. Surely you do not think for a moment that you would fail any more completely than you are failing by making no effort at all. Certainly to refuse to try is the supreme failure.

Now look what calamity was wrought for this man by scarecrows. Look what his fears did for him. First, they kept him from doing anything. I met a huge dog one day. This dog sprang at me and I did the wisest thing possible. I stood still in my tracks and looked at him. But the reason that I did so was not because I knew that such conduct was wise. I did so because I was literally frozen with fear. My fears

had me petrified. So it was with this man. He was
so afraid of doing the wrong thing that he did nothing.

The second calamity that it worked for him was that
it kept him from rendering any service. Other men
toiled for their master and increased their store from
two to four and from five to ten. But he never increased his in the slightest. He was no bigger at the
hour of his death than he was at his birth hour. He
never grew. He never helped. He never served in
the slightest degree. He began, continued and ended
utterly useless.

The final tragedy of his life was that he lost everything. "Take the talent from him," said the Master,
"and give it unto him which hath ten talents. For
unto every one that hath shall be given, . . . but from
him that hath not shall be taken away even that which
he hath." The penalty for not using that which you
have is to lose it. Darwin lost his taste for music
and poetry by simply refusing to use them. Many a
man has lost his brains in the same way, and far more
have lost their faith and their spiritual capacity.

Not only did this man lose his moral wealth, not only
did he lose his character, but losing that he of necessity lost his destiny. He was not commended by his
master simply because he was not worthy of commendation. He did not miss the joy of his lord because
his lord wanted him to miss it. He missed it because
he refused to take it.

But what is to be done with these scarecrows? We
cannot deny their existence. Our fears are very real.
There are some few people who are utterly blind to
scarecrows. They never see them. The bulldog is a
creature like that. He is scarecrow-blind. But most
of us are creatures tormented by many fears. We never

pass a garden without seeing a scarecrow. What shall we do with them?

First, make use of them. This very brilliant essayist says that if he were a bird he would make it his business to hunt for scarecrows. He would light on Church steeples and every high place he could find and look north, east, south and west for scarecrows. He would do this because a scarecrow is an indication of something desirable. Any intelligent bird ought to know that no man ever sets up a scarecrow in an untilled garden. Nobody ever saw a scarecrow in a desert. A scarecrow is a summons to a feast. It is as musical as a dinner bell. It is a grotesquely engraved invitation to a banquet.

So we are to use our scarecrows. The very fact that an enterprise is difficult is one indication, as a rule, of its desirability. If you want to drift, if you want to refuse to accept any kind of responsibility, that is easy enough. There are no forbidding specters to frighten you out of that path. But the minute you seek to count as you know you ought to count, there are hardships to be faced. To set yourself to be a Christian, for instance, is to face that terrifying scarecrow of self-denial. "If any man will come after me, let him deny himself." And yet this is a guide post to life, for it is only as we lose our lives that we truly find them.

Not only are we to use our scarecrows as guides to the most desirable gardens of life, but having accepted their guidance our next and final step is to defy them. It is useless for a scarecrow to tell that bird on yonder distant twig that it has strawberries at its feet unless the bird dares to face the horrid effigy and claim the berries. So you are to treat your scarecrows. You are afraid, of course. But do the thing you ought to do in spite of your fears. That is the highest type of courage.

At the close of this service you are going to have an opportunity to declare your faith in and your allegiance to Jesus Christ. It will tax your courage to the utmost. You may feel as if a thousand eyes are looking at you. It may seem as if the aisle down which you walk is almost a mile long. You will be afraid. But your very fears point toward the worthwhileness of the task. And if you will defy them you will gain a great victory and be only the stronger for the foes that you have had to overcome.

To such as defy their fears there is a wonderful discovery. These two blackbirds sitting the one on the right arm and the other on the left of this scarecrow have this to say to us, that scarecrows are utterly harmless things after all. They cannot hurt you in the least. They can only frighten you. And so it is with our worst fears. We are terribly afraid of ridicule, and yet ridicule could not hurt us. We dread criticism, but criticism could not kill. We dread death, but death is only a scarecrow.

It is said that when the Arena was finished in Rome the Emperor with many of the nobles met to celebrate its completion and also to do honor to the architect who had planned it. The Emperor made a speech stating that they had come together to celebrate the great achievement and the genius that had planned it, and that they were going to do so by throwing certain Christians to the lions. Now it so happened that the architect had been converted to Christianity just a few days before. When he heard this the Arena swarmed with scarecrows, the scarecrows of scorn, of disgrace, of death. But this brave man heeded them not, but calmly rose and said, "I am a Christian." And in less than five minutes he was torn to pieces. But he found that that grim scarecrow called "death" was only the guide to the eternal gardens of God. May you find victory tonight in the conquest of your fears.

IX

AN EASTER JOURNEY—CLEOPAS AND HIS COMPANION

Luke 24: 13-31

Hear the text: "Their eyes were opened and they knew Him." Thus it stands written of one Cleopas and his companion. Who this companion was we do not know. How well educated these two were is also unknown. But of this we are sure: they were in possession of the supreme knowledge. They knew Jesus Himself. Of course it is well to know about Jesus, but it counts for but little if we fail to really know Him. It is well to know theology, but that is a thoroughly dead and barren knowledge unless our eyes are open and we know Him. Botany is an exceedingly poor substitute for roses and violets. Astronomy can never take the place of the sun nor spill from its pages the pale light of stars. Just so no knowledge about Jesus is sufficient. We must come as did these two disciples of old to know Jesus Himself.

Now look at their story. It is the world's first glad Easter day. Jesus Christ has risen and has brought life and immortality to light. The tomb in Joseph's garden is empty. Death has been conquered and Jesus is abroad in a springtime world. But there are those who have companied with Him and who love Him well who do not know this. Here we see two of them, Cleopas and his companion, as they take their way

down the narrow streets of Jerusalem out the city gate
toward the village of Emmaus. They have passed over
this road in other days with fine hopes and high expectations. But something has happened since then
that has dashed all their hopes to the ground. They
are now broken-hearted, and they have decided to go
back home.

It is a great privilege to go home under certain con-
ditions. No doubt some of the gladdest moments of
our lives have been those moments when we turned
our faces toward home. There are memories of home-
goings in my own past that I can never forget. You
have such memories today and they are unspeakably
precious. You can never forget how the very car
wheels seemed to sing "Home, Sweet Home" as you
joyously journeyed toward those that you loved.

But there are other times when to go home is fraught
with deepest pain. It was so in this case, for these two
are going home from a new-made grave. They are
going home after the funeral. They are walking that
weary way that leads from the cemetery. What a
familiar way it is. How many leaden feet have walked
it. How many smarting eyes have bathed its dust
with tears.

It is a road that you have walked and I have walked,
and though faith in God and the passing years have
in some measure softened our grief, yet we cannot
think of that journey still without a strange clutching
at our hearts. We do not find it easy to go back to
the old life without the cheering fellowship of one
whom we had loved and lost. We keep toys with which
no baby plays. And when we look at them they remind
us of the one who is playing in the Nursery of Eternity.
We keep a little worn shoe and sometimes we sob over

it, not without a strange joy, because we are sure that
the little foot that used to wear it now walks amidst
the unfading gardens of God.

These people, I say, were going home from a new-
made grave, and for this reason they were sad. And
for this reason, too, we look upon them today with a
bit of sympathy and understanding because the road
they walked is in some measure so familiar to us.
We ourselves are in no sense strangers to its weary
leaden miles.

> "There's a magical isle up the River Time,
>   Where the softest of airs are playing;
> There's a cloudless sky and a tropical clime,
> And a song as sweet as a vesper chime,
>   And the Junes with the roses are straying.
>
> "And the name of the isle is the Long Ago,
>   And we bury our treasures there;
> There are brows of beauty and bosoms of snow;
> There are heaps of dust—but we loved them so!
>   There are trinkets, and tresses of hair.
>
> "There are fragments of song that nobody sings,
>   And a part of an infant's prayer;
> There's a lute unswept, and a harp without strings;
> There are broken vows, and pieces of rings,
>   And the garments that She used to wear."

But these two disciples had not only lost one whom
they loved, but they had also lost their Lord. They had
lost the One from whom they expected redemption.
They had lost the One who makes the funerals of our
own loved ones bearable. In fact it is hard to understand how people endure the separations of this life
unless they know something of the comfort and the
hope that is held out to us through our risen Lord.

There is something unspeakably sad in the epitaph
that America's greatest laugher wrote upon the tomb
of one he loved:

> "Warm summer sun, shine brightly here,
> Warm summer breeze, blow softly here,
> Green turf above, lie light, lie light.
> Good-night, dear heart, good-night, good-night."

There seems in it so little hope of an awakening. How
much better that gladsome song,—

> "Life, we have been long together
> Through pleasant and through cloudy weather.
> 'Tis hard to part when friends are dear,
> Perhaps will cost a sigh, a tear,
> Then steal away, give little warning,
> Say not good-night, but in some brighter clime
> Bid me good morning."

So it is a weary road that these two disciples travel
this Easter day. It is springtime, but for them no
flowers bloom and no birds sing. It is springtime, but
they walk under leaden skies, and their hearts are in
the freezing grip of winter. It is only seven miles to
Emmaus, but what a long, long way it seems. For they
are sad and they walk with lagging steps. And as they
walk they talk tearfully of the glad days "that have
dropped into the sunset." "Don't you remember," said
one to the other, "how He wept in the grief of Mary
and Martha? Do you remember how God-like He
seemed when He called Lazarus from the dead?"

"Yes, yes," came the answer, and it was mingled
with a sob. "I was sure that it was He who should
redeem Israel. I was perfectly confident that He was
the Christ. I never dreamed that death could conquer

Him just as it conquers other men. But alas and alas, they have crucified Him. So we must have misunderstood Him. But it is so hard to realize that we were mistaken in thinking that He was to be the world's Redeemer."

But when we look at them again they no longer walk alone. A winsome Stranger has joined them, and the three are now talking together. For be it said to the credit of these disciples that their conversation was of such a character that Jesus Himself could enter into it without embarrassment. All of our conversations are not pitched on so high a plane. "Jesus Himself drew near and went with them."

And, believe me, no lonely soul ever turns away from a new-made grave that Jesus is not there. But the tragedy of it is that we, just as these, so often fail to recognize Him. "Their eyes were holden that they should not know Him." And there they went, and they thought He was in the tomb. They remembered the great stone that lay across the grave. They could still see the red Roman seal upon it. It represented to them the impassable barrier that separated them from Him whom they had loved. Beyond that barrier their ministering hands could not go. Beyond that barrier their voices could not penetrate. Yet all the while Jesus was near. Jesus was with them, talking to them, longing to be recognized. What a loss to the disciples themselves. What a grief to Jesus. I think one of the hardest things that our Lord has to bear at our hands is just this, that we so often fail to recognize Him.

Why did they not know Him? The story says, "Their eyes were holden." But what caused that? What lay back of the blinded eyes? Just this: unbelief. They were not blind because Christ wanted them to be. Their eyes were put out by their lack of faith. You are aware of the fact that doubt looks upon faith as dull-eyed and credulous. You are aware of the fact that doubt flatters itself that it is broad-browed and keen-eyed. But the truth of the matter is that doubt is blinding. Doubt dulls our vision. This is true in all departments of life.

Faith looked at a drop of water once as it rose into steam. It saw in that little bit of vapor a prophecy of a power that would one day remake the world. Doubt saw only a passing vapor. Faith sees "earth crammed with Heaven and every common bush aflame with God," while doubt sits round and picks blackberries. Faith sees the horses and chariots of the Lord roundabout, while doubt sees nothing but encircling foes. There is nothing so bat-eyed as doubt.

But to these doubt-blinded disciples Jesus comes. He came to them because in spite of the fact that they doubted, they yearned for Him. They wanted to believe. They were hungry-hearted. And so He enters into conversation with them: "What communications are these that ye have one with another?" He did not ask that question for information. He asked it because He wanted to hear the story from their lips. Christ knew their hearts, but He wanted to be told of their love and of their grief. He is just that much like ourselves, and we are just that much like Him. Then, too, they needed to tell Him.

And so Cleopas began to tell Him. He told Him of the big hopes of yesterday. He told Him of the great dreams they had dreamed. He told Him of how winsome and of how mighty had been their young Prophet. And then in tones shaken with sobs he told Him of the awful happenings of last Friday. "Yes, we saw

Him nailed to the cross. We heard His wild cry, 'Why hast thou forsaken me?' We saw Him die. We saw Him laid in Joseph's tomb. So of course everything is lost because a crucified Messiah can never save the world.''

And you know what happened then? Jesus began to explain to them in all the scriptures the things concerning Himself. He opened up before their ignorant and doubt-blinded eyes the treasures of the Word of God. And mark you, He did not have a New Testament. He only had the Old. But "beginning with Moses and the prophets, He expounded unto them in all the scriptures the things concerning Himself."

Would it not have been wonderful to have heard the Inspirer of this Word explain it? There are those today who are ready to throw aside the Old Testament. But Jesus found it full of teaching about Himself. I can hear Him as He tells them how Moses had said that "a prophet shall the Lord God raise up unto you like unto me." He showed them how another had said, "Mine own familiar friend in whom I trusted has lifted up his heel against me." And He showed how this Messiah was to be sold. Then He came to that marvelous 53d chapter of Isaiah and expounded that to them:

"Who hath believed our report? and to whom is the arm of the Lord revealed? For he shall grow up before him as a tender plant, and as a root out of a dry ground: he hath no form nor comeliness: and when we shall see him, there is no beauty that we should desire him. He is despised and rejected of men; a man of sorrows, and acquainted with grief: and we hid as it were our faces from him; he was despised, and we esteemed him not. Surely he hath borne our griefs, and carried our sorrows: yet we did esteem him stricken, smitten of God, and afflicted. But he was wounded for our transgressions, he was bruised for our iniquities; the chastisement of our peace was upon him; and with his stripes we are healed. All we like sheep have gone astray; we have turned every one to his own way; and the Lord hath laid on him the iniquity of us all."

And as He opened unto them the scriptures, the burnt-out fires of hope kindled upon the altars of their souls. They saw not only that it was possible for the Christ to suffer, but also that the fact of His suffering was the supreme proof of His Messiahship. They saw also that just as the fact of His suffering was foretold, so His resurrection was foretold. And the road lost its weariness. It became a radiant road, and all too soon they found themselves at the door of their humble little home.

But the conversation has now become too fascinating to be broken into. They cannot let this winsome Stranger go. They fairly seize on to Him, saying, "Abide with us, for it is toward evening and the day is far spent." They are intensely in earnest and Christ never fails to come in where He is wanted. These people were eager for Him. They clung to Him. And Jesus responded. He went in. Is there not something marvelously beautiful in the fact that this great Lord who has just conquered death is not too great to walk along the dusty highway with two disciples, one of whom is nameless? Is it not marvelously comforting that He is great enough to enter into the humble home of these lowly people to share their hospitality. "He went in to tarry with them." That is what the story says.

And when they sat at the table He Himself assumed the place of host. That is what He always promises to do—"If any man will open the door I will come in and sup with him, and he with me." He took bread and gave thanks and broke it. "And their eyes were opened and they knew Him, and He vanished out of their sight."

Now, the big fact about this story, the important fact, is not how Jesus came to be known to these people. It is the fact that He really did become known to them. They came to know Jesus Himself, and that, I repeat, is the supreme knowledge. It is that without which all other knowledge comes to naught. They came to know Jesus as a living and risen and reigning Savior.

And this is the blessed experience into which Christ wants to lead every one of us on this Easter Sunday. For we are not to think for a moment that it is His will that He shall be unrecognized. Do not believe that He has nothing more to offer us this morning than cold evidences of His resurrection. There are evidences. But we want more than these. My hunger is an evidence of bread, but I need more than mere evidence to satisfy that hunger. My parched tongue is an evidence of water. But before my real need is met I must kiss a spring on the lips. He is saying, "Son, thou art ever with me and all that I have is thine." We may have the presence of Christ Himself as our comfort in our hours of sorrow. We may have Christ Himself as our defense in our hours of temptation. We may have Christ Himself as our antidote against fear in our hours of weakness and cowardice and failure.

When I was a small boy my father and I were overtaken while in the field by a terrible rain. Such a downpour I have seldom ever seen. As we made our

way home we found very tiny branches swollen into
big and mad streams. I walked behind. In one place
I stepped into father's track. The ground was soft and
the water began to rise about me. I was afraid and
cried for help. What I needed then was not evidences
of my father. I had that. I was standing in his very
tracks. I needed Father himself. I needed his strong
arms about me and that is just what he gave.

"They knew Him," and because they knew Him they
forgot their sorrow. Because they knew Him they forgot their weariness. Because they knew Him they forgot that the day was far spent. "They rose the same
hour and returned to Jerusalem." And how different
was the journey back to the city. They walked upon
feet made nimble and swift by a great joy. When they
reached Jerusalem they had "a sure word." They did
not indulge in speculations. They did not enter into
long arguments in defense of their faith. They simply
bore witness to a personal experience. They said, "Our
eyes were opened and we knew Him." May that
blessed knowledge be the portion of every one of us at
this glad Eastertide.

If we know Jesus, in the first place, we know that
we have a victorious Savior. No amount of the mere
letter of the law can bring to us this knowledge. No
man can call Jesus Lord but by the Holy Ghost. A
skeptic said to a sad-faced man in London once, "Do
you know Jesus?" And the man answered, "By the
grace of God, I do." And then the skeptic asked him
certain historic questions, and the man could not answer them. And his questioner replied with a sneer,
"You see you don't know Jesus as well as you thought."
"Yes, I do," replied the man. "I know that three years
ago I was the worst drunkard in the East End of

London, and I know that today I am saved and kept by the power of God. I know Jesus."

If you know this risen Christ then the grave is no longer a blind alley for you. "It is a thoroughfare. It is no longer a terminus. It is a highway." If Christ is to you a reality you no longer seek for the living among the dead, for you realize that the dead are alive forever more.

If you know the risen Christ, in the third place, you not only look upon an open grave, but you look upon an open Heaven as well. These people watched Jesus ascend a little later, and they returned to Jerusalem from that separation with great joy, for they were perfectly confident that the separation was only temporary. They were perfectly sure that He who had entered in through the gateway of cloud into the City Eternal had left the gate ajar, and that one day He was coming to receive them unto Himself that where He was, there they should be also.

And this is your hope and mine this glad Easter day. Believe it, Heart, Heaven's gate stands wide open for you and for me. Let us think gladly of it, for it may be our home. Let us think gladly of it, for it will bring us into the fellowship of those "we have loved long since and lost awhile." Let us think gladly of it because there "we shall see Him face to face and tell the story saved by grace." So my fondest hope for you and myself is this, that our eyes may be opened that we may know Him.

X

A FINE ANIMAL—ESAU

Genesis 25: 34; Hebrews 12: 16

In Genesis 25 : 34 we read these words: "And he did eat and drink and rose up and went his way: thus Esau despised his birthright." No doubt you are well acquainted with Esau. You know him of that far distant yesterday. You also know him of today. There is much that is admirable about him. He has many qualities that we frankly admire. He is possessed of characteristics that tend to make him welcome in the society of our day and of any day.

In the first place, Esau is a splendid animal. The tan of summer suns is upon his face. The strength and elasticity of many a mountain climb is in his limbs. He has the graceful and easy movements of the athlete. He is a fine, upstanding, husky fellow that makes a pleasing impression upon any crowd in which he chances to be.

Then he is possessed of a charming physical courage and daring. I do not think Esau would count for a straw on a moral stand, but physically he was unafraid. He has that type of courage which we admire, but which the bulldog possesses along with ourselves. In the chase he is ever the leader. In the places of danger he goes with a total unconsciousness of fear. He would have made an admirable man on the football team. He is rich in physical strength and courage.

In the next place he is generous and open-handed and open-hearted. He is quick to be angry and equally quick to make up. He would never stoop to do a mean and cowardly and ungenerous thing. He might despise his brother Jacob, but he would be too big to drive a sharp bargain with him as Jacob drove with himself. He is a breezy Bohemian type of man. He has a way of putting all his goods in the show case and thus often winning an applause that is not his due.

Now if you are a reader of modern fiction you have possibly been struck with the fondness of many of our present-day authors for the type of character that Esau represents. Did you ever notice with what delight many of our fiction writers picture the virtues of some worldling against the background of the failures and vices of some church man? It seems to be a most joyful pastime with a certain type of author. The name of such books is almost legion. Take "The Calling of Dan Matthews" for instance. The only three characters in there that the author would have us respect are an infidel doctor, a nurse who is a rank materialist and a preacher who is an utter coward and who gives up his Christ and his vocation for the love of a woman. Now there are folks that are like these, but they are not the folks who keep up the moral standards of the communities in which they live. Yet the author tries to make us believe that this is the case.

Or take a later book. Take the work of that literary scavenger who took a stroll down "Main Street." He is not without ability. But he is a self-appointed inspector of street gutters and of sewers. He has an eye for the moral carrion of the community. Now whom does he seek to have us respect? Who are the ones that when sickness comes do the self-forgetful and the self-sacrificing deeds of service? Not the people of faith. Not those who believe in Christ.

No, there are just two characters in the book that the author thinks are worthy of our admiration. There are only two who have fine, heroic qualities. One of them is a renegade Swede who is anchored to no place and who is mastered by no principles; a physical and a moral tramp. The other is a little bunch of feminine ignorance and conceit and ingratitude. She is the wife of the physician of the book. She is the one who plays the heroine when sickness comes to the Swede's house. But she sees nothing heroic in the common duties of life. She has no appreciation of her social relationships. As a wife she is a travesty and as a mother she is a cynical joke.

It is amazing why any intelligent author will show you beautiful effects when he paints behind these effects base and ugly causes. It is easy for an author to leave the impression that those who do the charitable work of the world are the irreligious. It is easy to paint the unbeliever as charitable and broad-minded and kind and the believer as uncharitable and narrow and mean. But when we get into the realm of fact we know that the picture is utterly false. There are mean men in the church, we are ready to confess. But they are not mean because of their Christianity. They are mean for lack of it, and to take any other position is to be dishonest. And yet tens of thousands are taken in by this dishonesty. And so there are vast multitudes who are antagonistic to the Church of Christ today because they do not know for what it stands.

Now while the type of character represented by this generous animal Esau may be made to look well in a piece of fiction, we must confess that he does not look

well here in the sacred record. It is true that Jacob
does not measure up either. His conduct is mean and
despicable. But with all his faults he is far more
hopeful than this breezy brother of his who sells his
birthright for a mess of pottage.

Look at the picture. Esau has returned from the
hunt. In the excitement of the day he has forgotten in
some measure his keen hunger. But now as he returns
his animal appetite clamors for immediate satisfaction.
As he comes to the tents of his people he is greeted by
the savory odor of the pot of lentils that his brother
Jacob is cooking. The fumes go to his brain like the
fumes of liquor to the brain of a toper. He must have
some of that food at once. So he lifts the flap of the
tent and shouts to his keen and watchful brother: "Let
me gulp down some of that red stuff."

Jacob sees his chance. He knows that Esau does not
set a great price upon his birthright. A man does not
come to despise his birthright all at once. He has heard
him speak of it jestingly, flippantly. He has heard him
make flings at it as a thing of no great value. For
this reason he believes that the time has come now that
he may win his desire.

"All right," he replies to his hungry brother, "I will
let you gulp down this red stuff. But first you must
sell me your birthright." Esau hesitates a moment,
scowls, breathes in the fragrant odor of the cooking
lentils and then with a snap of his finger says: "Take
it. What's the good of it anyway? Besides, I am
about to die and what good will a birthright do me if
I die of starvation?"

A moment later Esau is doing what he has requested
to do. He is gulping down the hot beans that Jacob
has sold him. He eats with rapidity and relish. At

last the large porringer is empty. Then Esau heaves a satisfied sigh, draws the sleeve of his goat-skin coat across his mouth, yawns, looks sleepily about him, rises and walks out of the tent and off the stage. "And he did eat and drink and rose up and went his way: thus Esau despised his birthright."

He ate and drank and went his way. That short sentence tells about all life meant to Esau. Almost his entire biography is written in that one brief sentence. And you cannot but be struck with what a mean affair it was. Suppose you wanted to dramatize the life of Esau. It would be an exceedingly simple matter. You would need only two articles of furniture on the stage: a dish of lentils and a coffin. It would not take a genius to play the part of Esau. A trained monkey would be sufficient. In fact, even a pig might serve. So simple is the part that any animal that is able to eat and walk and die might take it. "And he did eat and drink and rose up and went his way."

This is Esau's story and yet his grandfather was a man who was known as the friend of God. This is a story of one who had the same blood in his veins as that which flowed in the veins of Moses and of Paul. Yet how little life meant to him! How small was his achievement! I see him stumbling off the stage and I cannot but ask him a question. "Esau, you are going out into the night. You have lived your life. What have you accomplished? What has it meant to you? What has it meant to the world?"

When I ask Moses that question he can point to a nation that has been led from bondage to freedom. When I ask Paul he can point to nations that once sat in darkness that have come into the light. But when I ask Esau he can only point to an empty dish. And

he says: "Do you see that empty dish? When I began
to do business in this world that dish was full of beans,
steaming hot beans. It is empty now. That is what
I have accomplished. That is what life has meant to
me." "And he sat down to eat and drink and rose up
and went his way." What an awful failure he was!

Now what is the secret of Esau's failure? He did
not fail because he was vicious. He did not fail because he was mean and cruel. When we ask for the
answer to this question we find it in the letter to the
Hebrews. The writer of this letter lays two charges
against Esau. One of them is that he was a forni-
cator or better translated, that he was a sensualist, a
mere animal. The other charge against him is that he
was profane.

Take the first charge. Esau failed because he was
sensual. Now we have come to use this word today
with a restricted meaning. It refers to one form of
vice. But as used here it has a wider meaning. It
means that Esau lived his life in the realm of the
sensual. He was a slave to the visible, to the tangible,
to the physical. He had no sense or appreciation of
the spiritual and of the unseen. He lived his life upon
the same plane that he would have lived it if he had
been nothing more than an intelligent animal.

Being a sensualist Esau had no appreciation of his
own manhood. There are people who offend us because
of their self-satisfied conceit. There are people who
make us laugh because of the exalted opinion they have
of themselves. A gentleman came forward at the close
of a service recently and informed me that he would
certainly like to hear me preach if I knew what he
knew. And I thought that I would certainly like to
hear him if he only knew as much as he thought he

knew. Pure unmitigated conceit is offensive and laughable.

But, mark you, there is something far worse than conceit, and that is the despising of your own manhood. Scientists have been looking for the missing link between man and the lower animals for many years. But as a matter of fact, the whole chain is missing. There is a chasm between you and the best chimpanzee alive that is infinitely wider than the spaces between the stars. When I turn to the Record I read: "When I consider the heavens, the work of thy fingers, the moon and the stars which thou hast ordained, what is man that thou art mindful of him and the Son of man that thou visitest him? Thou madest him a little lower than God and crownedest him with glory and honour." When I read that I do not wonder that the world's greatest genius has exclaimed: "What a piece of work is man! How noble in reason; how infinite in faculty; in form and bearing how express and admirable; in apprehension how like an angel; in comprehension how like a God!"

This is not denying that man is a sinner. This is not shutting our eyes to the fact that there is much in us that is mean and ugly. We know that man has sinned. That in itself is an indication of his possible greatness. The beast cannot sin. He has no will. He is not made in the image of God. He is incapable of choice. Man has this Godlike capacity. Therefore he can take the lower road. He can plunge into the abysm of night if he will. But he can also home among the stars.

Now a man may fail because of a shallow self-conceit. A man may fail from overestimating himself. But where one fails by so doing, I am persuaded that scores fail from underestimating themselves. A contempt for yourself as a man is not the way to ascend unto the heights. There is some truth in Tennyson's statement: "Self-reverence, self-knowledge, self-control; these three alone lead to sovereign power." You may smile at the cynic who says: "I could believe in humanity if it were not for folks." But you have got to believe in and appreciate your own humanity or you will sink into the hell of the sensualist.

And if you find this hard, remember this, that Jesus Christ believed in humanity. As worthless as you seem to yourself sometimes, as worthless as the other man seems, there is something in the poorest of us that Jesus Christ thought of infinite value. Every man in His sight bore the image of Almighty God stamped upon him. But the sensualist has no appreciation of this. Therefore we are not surprised to hear the sensual Beau Brummell declare that the life of a dog is better than the life of a man.

Esau, having no appreciation of his own manhood, was devoid of self-control. There was no special reason why he should control himself. "Ye are the temple of the living God. As God hath said, 'I will dwell in them and walk in them.'" Again we read, "Know ye not that ye are the temple of God, that the spirit of God dwelleth in you?" A man that has this faith will realize the absolute necessity of a holy self-control and self-mastery. But without it we tend to yield to the inevitable outcome of sensuality.

You remember Esau is spoken of as a profane person. That does not mean that Esau swore. It is possible that he did. But it means that Esau had no "holy place" in his life. Pro—in front of, and fane—the temple. His life was outside. It was unfenced. It had no high wall of conviction about it. It was shut in by no iron grating of principle. Hence his soul became the galloping ground of any and every foul passion that desired to romp across it.

Being a sensualist Esau had no appreciation of his own possibilities. It never occurred to him to dream great dreams of the larger man he might become. In fact he was not interested in tomorrow. He was only interested in today. As long as examination day was next week Esau would never bother. The sensualist will not allow the future to interfere with what he wants to do in the present. He mortgages his to-morrow to his today.

"Esau, suppose you sell your birthright today, how about tomorrow? Did it ever occur to you that you might regret it some time? Did you ever stop to consider that you might one day be sorry? If you are never sorry in the world that now is, are you not afraid that you will miss something in the life that is to come?" And Esau is not interested in the least. If he is immortal he does not care to think about it. He says, "This present life is enough for me. I am willing to take the cash and let the credit go."

So he forgot that however poor a creature he was he was capable of being remade by the power of God. He forgot that he had the capacity for infinite growth and development. He ignored the fact that there were moral heights ahead of him that he might scale in the fellowship of the Most High. Being a sensualist he was not at all interested in the larger and finer and nobler character that he might achieve. Being a sensualist he was not concerned in the achieving of the Godlike character that God had made possible for him.

Just as Esau was not interested in being, neither was

he interested in doing. He belonged to the family that had entered into a covenant relation with God. He belonged to the privileged. But he had no sense of obligation. There were no compelling convictions that urged him on to service. Esau never said, "I must do this" or "I must do that." He simply said, "I will do as I please."

Esau had no appreciation of God nor of those eternal spiritual values that are represented by a truly religious life. Not that Esau hated religion. Not that he had for a moment thought of fighting the Church or tearing the Bible into shreds. The position of Esau on matters spiritual was just this: he cared nothing about them whatever. He was simply not interested. They had no place in his scheme of things. There are multitudes like him today, people who have no more interest in the Lord Jesus Christ than if they were highly intelligent animals and no more.

When I was a boy I had a dog to which I was greatly devoted. There were some things that we would enjoy together. If mother gave me a piece of bread I could share it with him and we could both enjoy it. If we were hunting we both found joy in chasing a rabbit or a squirrel. But there were places where our companionship stopped. When I memorized the Twenty-third Psalm he didn't enter into it with me. When I undertook to pray he stood by with no interest whatsoever. He did not growl nor bark nor bite on such occasions. He simply cared for none of these things. And on such a plane did Esau live his life.

Esau sold his birthright then because he was content to be only an animal. And it is interesting to notice the price that he got for it. What did Jacob pay him? He paid him one good square meal. That is all. "And

he sat down and ate and drank and rose up and went
his way." And when you see how cheaply this man
sold out you are ready to shout "Fool" at him across
the wide spaces of the years. But before you do that,
think of your own life and maybe you will not have to
shout. Maybe you can just whisper the word into the
ear of your own soul. Esau got a good square meal.
How much better have you been paid?

Frankly, as I know myself and others, as I read history, I am persuaded that Esau was as well paid as
the average. He got as much for his birthright as Lord
Byron did. I think he got quite as much solid enjoyment out of his bargain as did Napoleon. He got as
much real pleasure out of that meal as did the millionaire who dumped himself into the sea the other day.
He had sold his birthright for a few millions of dollars.
And I seriously doubt if he had found as much pleasure in his millions as Esau found in his lentils.

But there came a time when Esau was dissatisfied
with the trade that he had made. That comes in every
life. No man can be satisfied with a sensual life, because he is more than a mere animal. I find no indication that the hogs among which the prodigal found
himself were unhappy or disconsolate hogs. The pigsty and the husks satisfied them quite well. As long
as they were fed they were content. They neither worried about yesterday nor today nor tomorrow. But
while they grunted restfully, the pangs of hell got hold
on the Prodigal. He could not forget that he was
made for something better. He was tormented by un-
satisfied hungers. He was tortured by unquenched
thirsts. He could not brush the loving face of his
father out of his mind. He could not banish the fellowships of home from his memory. He could far less

be at home there than an eagle could be at home in a cage of vultures.

So there came a day when Esau was sorry. "Afterward when he would have inherited the promise he found no place for repentance." Afterward—take that word in your hands and look at it. Read the story of his tragedy and of his tears. "Afterward." Esau shut his eyes to an afterward. He forgot that he had a future. But every act has an afterward, every good act and every sinful act. Let us not forget that.

"Afterward." When you sin you seek to say to that sin: "Be gone! I am through with you." But that sin turns and with a fiendish laughter says, "Yes, you would like to be through with me, but I am not through with you." Judas betrayed his Lord, but there was an afterward. David wronged Bathsheba and murdered her husband, but there was an afterward. Esau sold his birthright, but there was an afterward. One day he saw the value of what he had thrown away. One day he realized the man that he once could have been, but now cannot be. Afterwards when he had thrown away his chance he realized its value and found no place for repentance, though he sought it diligently and with tears.

Now this does not mean that Esau found no place for pardon. God will pardon us if we come to Him in the last minute of life. But there is one thing that even pardon cannot do. It cannot restore to us what our sin has thrown away. For instance, I talked this week to a poor, misguided mother who was dying from poison that she had taken with her own hands. She was sorry. She sought pardon at the Throne of Grace for the terrible sin she had committed. She had been a pitiful sufferer and I leave her with confidence in the hands of our merciful Savior. If we repent in our last moment God will save.

But there are some things that even repentance cannot do. Repentance for this poor woman could not restore her to health. It could not take the poison out of her tortured body. It could not give her back to the husband whose heart she had broken and to her motherless children.

To you who are living as Esau lived, not vicious, not cruel and full of hate, but only living for the things seen, you may repent of your bartered birthright some day. Should you repent at the last moment of life God would save you. What God could not do would be to put you where you were before you sinned, before you threw away your opportunity. Therefore the only wise thing to do is to repent now. Repent while you have something to give. Repent while the best years of your life are yet ahead of you. Give yourself now to the things that abide and are eternally worth while. For God can never restore to you the opportunities of this present moment.

"The moving finger writes, and having writ moves on;
　Nor all your piety nor wit can lure it back to cancel half
　　a line;
　Nor all your tears wash out a single word of it."

"Therefore today if you will hear His voice harden not your hearts."

XI

THE MODERN SLAVE—MARTHA

Luke 10: 41

"Martha, Martha, thou art anxious and troubled about many things." This is a domestic scene. It is exceedingly easy to reconstruct it. Unexpected company has come to the little home in Bethany. It is quite evident that these guests were unexpected from the simple fact that had Martha known that they were coming she would have prepared for them in advance. But they have come unannounced. One of them is exceedingly important. He is a great favorite with the whole household. His presence demands that a worthy feast be set.

This family that lived at Bethany is one of the famous and favorite families of the Bible. It is composed of three members: a brother, Lazarus, and two sisters, Martha and Mary. Martha is evidently the elder sister, and since the death of her mother her competent hands have guided the affairs of the house with thorough-going ability. "Had Martha gone on a visit Lazarus would have been a bit uneasy. Had Mary gone he would have been quite lonely."

No sooner had Martha greeted her guests than she disappeared. You know where she has gone. She has hurried off into the kitchen. Immediately there is the clatter of pans and the noise and bustle of an eager and competent cook. Soon we catch the savory odor of various dishes that she is preparing for the coming

128

meal. Now and then she hurries to the door to look out, as if she is expecting someone.

From one of these errands I can imagine she turned quickly, for there is the odor of something burning. By this time she is thoroughly worried and out of patience. "Why in the world," she mutters, "doesn't Mary come?" She will endure her neglect no longer. She hurries out of the kitchen into the parlor. There she sees her sister comfortably seated at the feet of Jesus and she is thoroughly out of patience with both of them, and proceeds to give expression to her displeasure.

"Master, dost thou not care that my sister has left me to serve alone? Bid her therefore that she help me." It is easy to see that this older sister is thoroughly exasperated. What her tone implies is about this: "Why should Mary sit still and talk while I do all the work? I would like to be in here myself, but it is necessary that somebody get dinner. I must take the lead in that, but it seems to me that the least that Mary could do would be to lend a hand. And I want you to send her on so that she can help."

Now it is impossible not to sympathize with Martha in some measure. We feel that her speech is quite natural and that her impatience is quite reasonable. But the rebuke that she expected Mary to receive was never given. Christ did not turn to Mary and say: "Mary, I am surprised at you. Go quickly and help Martha with the dinner." Instead of rebuking Mary He rebuked Martha. Instead of sending Mary away He said: "Martha, Martha, thou art anxious and troubled about many things. But one thing is needful and Mary hath chosen that good part, which shall not be taken away from her."

Some have been greatly perplexed over this rebuke. Some have tried to soften it so it would not be a rebuke at all. But there is no mistaking the fact that Jesus is not pleased with Martha. No doubt He spoke to her in great tenderness. But He spoke also in great earnestness, for He saw that His friend Martha was in real danger. He saw that she had a genuine need of this tender and timely word of warning.

Why did He rebuke Martha? What was there in her conduct that was deserving of this reproof? It was not that Martha was a wicked woman. She was not. She was a fine and true and noble woman in every respect. I doubt if there was a woman in her village who had more good deeds to her credit than did this busy and bustling woman Martha.

Neither did Jesus rebuke her because of her lack of devotion to Himself. Martha loved Jesus. There is no mistaking that. She is the one who is reported as receiving Him into her house. Martha was in charge. If she had been a mind to she could have kept Jesus from coming at all. But though His presence made her unpopular, though His presence caused her house to be greatly criticized, yet for love's sake she dared the criticism and hatred of the best people of her day in order to give herself the pleasure of entertaining Jesus. She was a lover of Jesus and Jesus loved her. When John tells their story he mentions His love for Martha even before His love for Mary.

Nor did Jesus rebuke Martha because she was active and industrious. He did not rebuke her because she was a practical and earnest worker. Jesus was Himself a thoroughly practical man. He did not come to establish in the world an impossible scheme of things. It is true that men have looked upon Jesus as impractical. They have classed Him among the beautiful dreamers. So the statesmen have done. They themselves have gone on being practical till they have plunged the world into a veritable abysm of bloodshed and confusion, whereas if they had only followed the teaching of Jesus Christ there would have been long since a reign of brotherhood around the world.

Jesus, therefore, is not against the practical and common sense. He knows that folks must have dinners. He knows that while people have souls they also have bodies. He is not a man of the cloister. He grew to manhood in a large family of not less than seven brothers and sisters, and he lived His life in the thick of things. He was an entirely practical worker. And the individual who is a dreamer of dreams and no more, receives no encouragement from Him.

Why, then, does He rebuke this practical and active and industrious woman Martha. The reason becomes clear, I think, when we listen attentively to what He says to her: "Martha, Martha, thou art anxious and troubled about many things." He is not rebuking her because she has to do with things. He is rather rebuking her because she is becoming the slave of the things with which she has to do. She is being threatened with what another has aptly called "the tyranny of things."

Life has become far more complicated since Martha lived. What a complex civilization is this of your day and mine! If the tyranny of things was a danger in Martha's day it is a far greater danger in the strenuous day in which we live. Slavery in the old sense has passed away, but how many slaves there are still! What countless thousands there are in the Church and out of the Church that are living today in the slavery of things.

What is the danger of this form of slavery? A danger it is. That fact is evident from the evils it is already working in the life of this good woman Martha. Look what disaster it was bringing to her. She was so occupied with things that she did not have any time to sit at the feet of Jesus. She was so enslaved by things that she was not free to hear His voice and drink in His wisdom. She was so busy that she had no time for the cultivation of the divine friendship and of the divine fellowship. She was working for Him, I know, but it is possible to even do that and at the same time forget Him. "You may be engaged about holy tasks and lose the fellowship of the holy Lord."

There was never a time when that danger was greater than now. We are so busy. We are so hurried and harassed. We are so overworked. This is one of the dangers of the modern minister. He is tempted to squander himself in many different directions. He is in danger of becoming a slave to the very routine of his work. There is a persistent danger of his becoming a slave to the mere externals of his vocation.

This danger dogs the steps of the business man. His business life is so strenuous that it tends to drink up his energy. On Sunday he is too tired to attend church and must find relaxation in bed, at tennis or on the golf links. Even if he attends church he is too preoccupied to receive any special spiritual enrichment.

This is one of the perils of our young people, especially here in Washington. There are a great many among us who are making really heroic efforts in order to obtain an education. They work during the day and go to school at night. Often we hear of a nervous breakdown. Where this physical collapse has not come there is often a moral collapse. Life is too crowded. We are cumbered with much serving. We are robbed of our needed quiet hour for the cultivation of the divine fellowship. Such slavery also creates a demand for a relaxation correspondingly intense.

Did you ever live on the farm? If you have you know what happens when you let out of the stable a mule that has been pent up for quite a long time. He has a tendency to run wild. And there is that, especially in an overworked young life, that makes that individual have a tendency also to run wild. If you ever get to the place where you feel as if you want to do something mean, that you are downright tired of being good and decent and respectable, that means that you are trying to rebel against your self-imposed slavery. Your soul is trying to get free from the bondage of things and it often seeks that freedom in the realm of license rather than of liberty. Martha allowed her slavery to things to rob her of the sense of the divine presence. It is possible for you and me to make the same tragic blunder.

Thus brought into bondage to things Martha did not find peace and joy. She loved Jesus. She was a Christian, but she was far from being a happy Christian. Hear what Jesus said to her: "Thou art anxious and troubled about many things." She was a thoroughly worried woman. Her heart was brimful of anxiety. Her face was lined with care. "Thou art anxious and troubled about many things." "Martha, let me congratulate you on having Christ as your guest." But when I get a good look at her face I hesitate. There is far more of sadness and of anxiety pictured there than of joy and peace.

Bondage to things always makes for worry. Your

chances for happiness are exactly in proportion to the things you can get along without. You remember that marvelous palace in "Arabian Nights." The owner was showing a friend over it, and that friend told him that all that he lacked was a roc's egg to swing from the ceiling. The owner did not know where to find this treasure and so the palace lost all of its charm. There is ever something wanting to the man who is a slave to things. As his wealth increases, just so swiftly and far more do his desires increase.

There is no doubt that Martha had a reputation for hospitality. She was proud of her reputation. But it is evident from the story that she did not so much possess her reputation as her reputation possessed her. She became its slave. It drove her to utter weariness and exhaustion. It harassed her and worried her and made her fretful and unhappy.

You have a position in society. You have a reputation for always doing the right thing at the right time. There was a day when your wants were very simple. But as time has passed you have made what the world terms a success and now you have to give a great many entertainments. You have to go to parties that do not interest you. You have to make scores of calls in which there is very little friendship. You have to attend social functions that are a weariness to the flesh and that bore you to the point of desperation. You think you have a position in society, but your position in society has you. You are its bondslave.

You have worked hard. You have succeeded. You congratulate yourself this morning that you own a good business. But in that I fear you are mistaken. In reality your business owns you. This summer I saw two flies walking along beside a ten-acre field—at least it looked like that to them. It was a lovely piece of fly-paper.

"What do you think of this new invention called Tanglefoot?" said the younger to the older. "I am opposed to it," was the instant reply. "How is that?" asked the younger fly. "I thought you were broad-minded. Is it poisonous?" "No," replied the other. "Is it bitter?" "No," came the reply again, "it is rather sweet." "Then what is your objection?" Just then a neighbor of theirs flew and lit down right in the center of the paper. "My objection," said the old fly, "is just this: you will never see our friend yonder in prayer meeting again. He thinks he owns the fly-paper, but the fly-paper owns him."

Maybe you are the preacher. You also have your reputation to look out for. You must therefore be sparkling and up-to-date. You must also know all about the latest consensus of modern scholarship. You must be so absorbed in preaching fine sermons that you fail to live a fine life. You must be so careful to say nice things about Jesus that you haven't time to get on intimate and living terms of fellowship with Jesus Himself.

Not only was Martha worried. She was actually ill-tempered. She got angry. And when her anger was blown away a little she was doubtless humiliated and ashamed of it. This shame made her all the more angry and worried and wretched. With Christ in her home she was a thoroughly dissatisfied and unhappy woman.

N. B.

If you are a bondslave to things you need not expect to find happiness. It does not come that way. "Give me health and a day," said Emerson, "and I'll make the pomp of emperors ridiculous." And many have made this pomp ridiculous even without the health. But no man has ever found happiness in things. Solomon had a lot of things, but he was terribly short on happiness. The Rich Fool had a tremendous amount of things, but no joy.

N. B.

How much more the modern child has to make him happy than did the child of only a few years ago. What a vast variety of toys is put at his disposal. He has them of every conceivable kind and value. This is not true simply of the rich. And yet I doubt if the modern child gets any more out of his toy organs and pianos and baby victrolas than we used to get out of a whistle made of a goose quill. I seriously doubt whether he gets any more joy out of all his toys that are made of wood than we used to get out of a top that was made of half a spool. Things do not make happiness. Slavery to things simply kills happiness.

Then Martha was not only worried and irritable and unhappy herself, but her influence in the household was bad. She cast the gloom of her worry and ill temper over others. She tried to entangle others in the same galling bondage from which she herself was suffering. Had she had her way she would have called her sister from the presence of Jesus Christ Himself. If I am a bondslave of things I tend to lead others into the same bondage.

This tendency accounts for many a disaster. One man in a certain circle begins to live beyond his income. And oftentimes a foolish neighbor of his will follow his example. One girl puts on finery for which she cannot legitimately pay. And her friend is enticed into the same madness. One young man spends beyond his earnings and his friend mistakes his folly for wisdom and gets caught in the same net. Thus bondage to things makes for our own slavery and for the slavery of others.

I am told that in the steamboat days of the Mississippi two steamers set out from New Orleans to Memphis. They belonged to rival companies, so they began to race. One of them carried a cargo of hams. It was discovered that a ham mixed with the coal now and then increased the heat and therefore the speed. This boat won the race, but it burned up its cargo on the way.

That is a parable. How many there are today that are spending so much in an effort to live that they are failing to lay hold on life. What is life for? It is given to us that we might lay hold on the pearl of great price. It is given us that we might attain the knowledge of God, Christlike character, high and holy service. But many of us are going to come to the end of the journey in the sad realization that we have burned up our cargo on the way.

What is the cure for this slavery to things? How shall we escape this galling tyranny? Mary shows us the way. How did she escape? There is nothing of the anxiety in her face that we find in the face of Martha. What is her secret? Answer: She chose the good part. She chose the fellowship of Jesus Christ Himself. That high choice saves us from the dominion and the slavery of things. As the sun puts out the stars, the rising of the Son of Righteousness in our hearts delivers us from the dominion of all inferior gods.

Having Him we have no fear of the loss of the things that we really need. "The Lord is my shepherd, I shall not want." That is a declaration of independence. That declares our independence, not of God, but our independence of things. It is said in firm faith that

God will supply all our needs according to His riches in glory. I had an old friend some years ago who was a very poor man so far as this world's goods are concerned. He had cultivated a crop of cotton on a piece of rented land. A terrible drouth came. He told me of going out into his cotton patch and seeing the blossoms raining upon the ground. He said, "I am not going to make a thing on that cotton. But I stood there and praised God. I said, 'Lord, I thought you were going to take care of me by means of this cotton, but it seems you are not. You have some other arrangements. I do not know what they are, but I know that you have made them. The Lord is my Shepherd, I shall not want.'"

A firm grip of Jesus Christ will also save us from the bondage of the lust of things that we cannot have. My God will supply all your needs, but beyond that He does not promise to go. He will teach us, as another has said, that it is better to desire what we have than to have what we desire. Some folks cannot enjoy looking at lovely things they are so eaten up with covetousness. How much freer is the sainted Bud Robinson. You remember the story of how he spent a day looking over the wonderful sights of New York only to return to his hotel at night to get down on his knees and say, "Lord, I just want to thank you that I haven't seen a single thing that I want."

A man thus set free can really find enjoyment in things. He can do so because he is independent of them. Those who are slaves to things cannot find such joy. It is only as you make things your servants by the grace of God that you can find the highest joy in them. It is altogether possible that there was a far better dinner served in the Bethany home that day than would have been served if Martha had been like Mary. But this is also quite true: there would have been far more enjoyment of the simple meal that Mary served than there was of the elaborate spread at the hands of Martha. Did Martha enjoy her own dinner? Certainly not. She was too worried and angry and tired and ashamed of herself. Did Christ enjoy Martha's dinner? No. He saw that His presence was making for trouble and annoyance rather than for helpfulness and happiness and peace. He saw that He was in the way. Did Mary enjoy it? No. Martha's rebuke had no doubt made her feel ill at ease and embarrassed. So that however good the dinner was that Martha had prepared it was a very poor affair after all.

So our Lord is calling us to simplicity. He is also calling us to freedom. "But one thing is needful." "Seek ye first the kingdom of God and His righteousness and all these things shall be added unto you." This does not mean that if you put God first you will get rich, but it does mean that if you put God first you will get what life needs. It means that if you put God first you will be set free from the galling tyranny of things. "For if the Son of God shall make you free you shall be free indeed." May the Lord help us to claim our birthright even as did this sainted woman Mary of the long ago.

XII

A GREAT WOMAN—THE SHUNAMMITE

II Kings 4: 8

"And it fell on a day that Elisha came to Shunem where there was a great woman." I like this wonderful Word of God. It is so sincere. It is so absolutely reliable. It is so truly trustworthy. When it utters a rebuke you know it is a deserved rebuke. Likewise, when it compliments, you know that the compliment has been worthily given. It is no fulsome flatterer, this Holy Book. It speaks the straight, plain truth, like a loyal and sincere friend.

Now there are a few individuals that give me considerable annoyance. One of them is the dill-pickle type. He prides himself on his power to find fault. Like Iago, the greatest devil of literature, he is nothing if not critical. He fixes his eye on the one wrong thing in your personal appearance, in your conversation, in your domestic life, in your church life. He believes that a cocklebur is more pleasing than a rose petal, and that the most delightful of animals is the porcupine.

Then there is that opposite type—the man who is always soft-soaping. He sows compliments broadcast as a farmer sows his grain. He is forever petting and coaxing and booing and cooing at you as if you were a baby. Now I like to be complimented. So do you. If you say you do not the only difference between you and me is that I tell the truth. But there is such a thing as putting it too strong. I do not mind in the least folks saying lovely things about me when those things are not true. That happens often. But I do desire to feel that they are foolish enough to think them true. But you cannot feel that way about the persistent flatterer. He is just too sweet. I like bonbons, but I do not care to sop them in honey.

One day I met this preacher Elisha and his assistant pastor. They were on a weary stretch of road winding down towards Shunem. The sun was beginning to turn the western hills to gold. "Good evening, Brother Elisha. Come home, you and your assistant, and spend the night with me." "No, thank you," he replies, "I am going to spend the night at Shunem." "Why," I say, "isn't that several miles down the road?" "It is." "Aren't you tired?" "I am." "Aren't there any houses between here and there where you might find shelter?" "Doubtless. Still," he says, "I am going to Shunem. I am going for the simple reason that there is a great woman down there who gives me shelter, and who makes me feel at home."

Wherein is this woman great?—for great she is. Do not forget that. God does not make mistakes when He writes the biographies of His characters, as men do. I turned over in some man-made history and read about a brilliant genius who utilized his great powers for the conquering and murdering of men. I read about one who turned half the world into a shamble. I read about a man who allowed his appetite to take him by the nape of his kingly neck and push his mouth down to the bung-hole of a keg, and make him drink himself to death. And this historian said that the man who did that was Alexander the Great.

The Bible would never blunder like that. It never confuses the real with the counterfeit. It never takes the tinsel for real gold. It calls this woman great because great she really was. But why? Wherein did her greatness lie? Why was she singled out from all those who lived about her, and made immortal, while they dropped into utter oblivion?

It is not hinted that her greatness lay merely in her physical charm. It is fine to be beautiful. I think it is our duty to be just as charming and just as beautiful as we can possibly be. Even then there is a possibility that some of us would not be conspicuous. But some of the most beautiful women I have ever known have been thorough pygmies. Cleopatra was beautiful, but you could not call her great.

Neither did this woman's greatness consist of her high social position. The place of leadership in society is in the minds of some a very desirable something. Yet it is possible to attain such a position, and then be very far from great. Lady Hamilton was a social success, but she was a moral dwarf. In the eyes of her own circle she looked large; through the microscope of Calvary she was smaller than the motes that people the sunbeam.

Nor was this woman called great because of her intellectual brilliancy. I am not accusing her of being stupid. My private opinion is that she was intellectually gifted. But greatness of intellect does not necessarily include greatness of soul. You may have a mind that flashes like a meteor, but its light may be only the baleful light of the star called Wormwood. This woman's greatness was greatness of soul. It was moral greatness. We can read this fact in the story of her life purpose.

What was that purpose? She was an ambitious woman. What was her ambition? It was not merely to live in pleasure. She knew that the woman who liveth in pleasure is dead while she liveth. Her ambition was not to make a career for herself in the great outside world. It is all right for some women to have such a career. I am not saying for a moment that God expects every woman to occupy the position of wifehood and motherhood. All honor to those brave women who have wrought mightily and helpfully on the great world stage. But this woman's ambition did not lead in that direction. Her life purpose was just this: to make a home.

Now you remember that she lived a long time ago. She lived long before the present-day emancipation of woman. In her day woman's sphere was very circumscribed. Today women may succeed in any vocation. But even bearing these facts in mind, we are convinced beyond a doubt that this great woman, dwelling in the little village of Shunem, chose the highest possible vocation that was open to women in her day, or in any other day. And I am persuaded, also, that with this old-fashioned faith most of you agree.

This is true because the home is the place of supreme influence and supreme power. This nation of ours is of tremendous importance. It has come to us at a great price. We ought to honor it more than we do. We ought to respect its laws as we do not respect them. We ought to seek to keep our great flag stainless. But there is an institution more fundamental and more important than the nation itself.

The Church of God is tremendously important. So important is it that it was purchased by the precious blood of Christ. The task of the building of the church is big enough to occupy the energies of the eternal God. "I will build My church, and the gates of Hell shall not prevail against it." It is to be the light of the world and the salt of the earth. Wherever the Church of God is weak, morality is weak. Wherever the Church of God loses her power, civilization rots down.

But there is an institution among us that is even more fundamental than the Church. It is more fundamental because it is the maker of the Church as it is the maker of the nation. That institution is the home. The home is the fountain from which flow the streams that make the great Mississippi of our national life and of our church life. As the streams are, so will be the great river. If we have today a growing number of lawless bootleggers among men, and liquor sippers and cigarette smokers among women, it is because we have raised them. And if tomorrow we are to have a Christian nation, and if tomorrow we are to have a Christian Church, we must have Christian homes today.

The home is, therefore, the most important institution in the world. To be queen here is to be queen of the vastest empire in existence. To rule rightly here is to rule aright everywhere; and to fail here is to fail everywhere. Hence, this woman showed her greatness when she was able to pass by the secondary in order to give her heart and her all to the accomplishing of the primary. She showed her greatness when she made it her one purpose to be the greatest blessing that can come to any community or to any world, a real home-builder.

Then this woman was great in her devotion to her task. There came a time when she was married. She did not do anything extra in marrying, but that is a very common occurrence. I have known other women who would be truly able to enter into sympathy with her. Her husband did not amount to so very much. But in spite of that she never faltered in her devotion. When opportunity came she was not to be turned aside. "Shall I speak for you to the king or to the captain of the hosts?" said her great preacher friend one day. "No," she replied, "I dwell among mine own people. I am sufficiently protected. I count it my highest duty as well as highest privilege to be the wife of a humble farmer, and to make for him a home."

And notice, will you, how she made this home. Her first step in making a home was that she lived there. Her home was her dwelling place. That sounds trivial, utterly trite. Still you must realize that one of the greatest dangers of today is that folks have stopped living at home. Home is a sleeping place. It is a place where you slip in and dress. It is a place where you come to spill out your bad temper that you have kept pent up during the day. But you do not dwell there. That is the reason it has ceased in a large measure to be home to you, and that is the further reason you have ceased to love home.

"Home ain't a place that gold can buy or get up in a minute;
  Afore it's home there's got t' be a heap o' livin' in it;
  Within the walls there's got t' be some babies born, and then
  Right there ye've got t' bring 'em up t' women good, an'
      men;
  And gradjerly as time goes on, ye find ye wouldn't part
  With anything they ever used—they've grown into yer
      heart;
  The old high chairs, the playthings, too, the little shoes they
      wore
  Ye hoard; an' if ye could ye'd keep the thumb-marks on
      the door.

"Ye've got t' weep t' make it home, ye've got t' sit and sigh,
  And watch beside a loved one's bed, an' know that Death
    is nigh;
  An' in the stillness o' the night t' see Death's angel come,
  An' close the eyes o' her that smiled, an' leave her sweet
    voice dumb.
Fer these are scenes that grip the heart, an' when yer tears
    are dried,
Ye find the home is dearer than it was, an' sanctified;
An' tuggin' at ye always are the pleasant memories
O' her that was an' is no more—ye can't escape from these.

"Ye've got t' sing an' dance fer years, ye've got t' romp an'
    play,
An' learn t' love the things ye have by usin' 'em each day;
Even the roses 'round the porch must blossom year by year
Afore they 'come a part o' ye suggestin' someone dear
Who used t' love 'em long ago, an' trained 'em jes' t' run
The way they do, so's they would get the early mornin' sun;
Ye've got t' love each brick an' stone from cellar up t'
    dome;
It takes a heap o' livin' in a house t' make it home."

It is this heap o' livin' that makes home the best
loved spot in all the world. "Home, Sweet Home"
was not born of the memory of a club. "How dear to
my heart are the scenes of my childhood," was not inspired by the memory of a palace in which we live for
six weeks of the year. These songs and these loves
spring out of the memory of an abiding place, a place
where mother lived, and wrought, and loved. And,
mark me, there is no home without this abiding. I
used to see a little child play from house to house on
the streets while her mother was away auto riding with
a man who was not her husband. That child has a
house to sleep in, but she has no home.

Down in the heart of the hills of Tennessee stands

an old-fashioned white house. There are sturdy apple trees still standing in front of it. They are great bouquets of color at this moment. The templed hills lift their tall heads above it. The forest of beech, oak, and chestnut stretches away in the distance back of it. The Buffalo River sings its sweet silver song just behind yon rim of trees. Little has changed since I was a child. But I do not go back there any more because the father and mother who made the home are not living there now. They are in God's house. Home is a place where somebody lives; above all it is a place where mother lives.

And this great woman was a devoted mother in heart long before she actually held her child in her arms. For years it looked as if the big dream of her life was never to be realized. For long she was childless. For long she waited for the little lad who did not come. But, denied the privilege of mothering her own child, she mothered the needy ones about her, because she had a mother-heart. Here was a tired preacher and his assistant, and she built a special room just for them. And what an artist she was at entertaining! To get down to her house was like getting home. It was like revelling in a day of bright sunshine after weeks of cloudy weather. It was like bursting into springtime after a long winter. It was like kissing a laughing spring on the lips after being choked by the sands of the desert.

Such a privilege it was to be in this home that the preacher felt he must make some return. But this strange woman did not care to be spoken for to the king or to the captain of the hosts. Then what did she like, asked the Prophet, and the wise assistant whispered in his ear: "She has no child." Ah, there was the sore spot. There was the wound that would not heal. There was the dream that had never materialized. There was the hope long deferred, that was making the heart sick. This woman yearned to be a mother. She wanted to feel the hugging of baby arms and the kiss of baby lips. She wanted to hear the music of baby prattle. And when the boon was promised, she felt that it was almost too good to be true.

But the great day came. The sweet angel of suffering visited the little home in Shunem and the most wonderful little laddie that ever lived was lying warm in her arms. He grew apace. One day he uttered a mysterious noise and she said he was calling "Daddy." And when he began to toddle about the house getting into everything, pulling out every drawer, spilling everything on the floor that he could spill, when he began to ask questions, questions that no philosopher on the face of the earth could answer, she only loved him the more.

He is quite a big lad now. He is big enough to go to the field with Daddy. It is harvest time. The day is hot. The oriental sun shines with greatest intensity. Suddenly the lad puts his hand to his forehead and says: "Oh, my head, my head!" The lad is sick, very sick. And the father is very helpless. He does not know what to do. "Take him to his mother," he says to one of his servants. Of course. That is where you always send those who are in trouble. That is where those who have aching heads and aching hearts almost always want to be sent. "Take him to his mother." Where is there another pillow so soft as her breast? Where is there a bed in all the world so comforting as her lap? Where is there such another physician as

mother? Where is there such healing in a touch and
healing in a kiss, surpassing all the remedies that
science ever dreamed of?

And what did this mother when the little lad came
with his aching head? She said, "I am sorry, but I
am just preparing to go out. I will send the nurse in
to look after him." That is what one mother said not
long ago. Her little daughter complained, and she
said, "I have an engagement at a bridge party. I
simply cannot fail to go." And she turned the little
girl over to the tender mercies of a servant. When she
came home late that night the little sufferer, cold and
ivory pale, lay on her bed asleep. She died, and she
died alone. She died without her mother. And in the
heart of that mother a poison dagger is buried, but no
surgeon has skill to extract it.

Not so, this mother! Not so, thank God, most
mothers! We read the story so human and so touch-
ing, and it tells that he sat on her knees until noon
and then died. But he died in his mother's arms. And
where is there a place more fitting? And where is there
a place that so robs death of its sting? He sat on her
knees until noon, and mother fought with death. She
contested every inch of the battle-field. She never even
took time to weep until the little fellow was gone. She
was too busy trying to defend him from the darts of
death.

But even when he was dead she did not give him up.
That is remarkable. Truly she was a great woman.
She was great in her faith. Somehow she had become
convinced that this lad of hers was God's lad. He had
come into her arms as a gift. She believed that her
God was mighty to overcome all foes. She believed,

even in that distant day, that with Him nothing was impossible. And so when hope was gone she kept on hoping.

Look at the picture. The little sufferer in her arms no longer moves. The lips are still. The heart is still. The eyes are still. All is still. And yet there is no wild cry of despair. With resolute face she mounts to the Prophet's room, lays the dead lad upon the Prophet's bed, and hurries off to continue her fight for the salvation of her boy. She does not send a servant to the Prophet. She goes in person, and with resolute faith that takes no denial she wins a victory. At the close of the day she is holding her little lad in her arms once more.

Oh, this is a story for every mother, and for every father too. This mother fought with death. She did all that was in her power to keep her child from ever going into that land of gloom. She did her best to prevent it. That, after all, is the greatest work of a mother and the greatest work of a home. How many of us present this morning have never tasted moral death, not because of the goodness inherent in ourselves, God knows, but because we have been prevented by the prayers of a saintly father and mother. They have defended us behind the protecting walls of a Christian home.

And then, how many who have gone into sin have been brought back by the unconquered faith and love and devotion of a holy mother! Oh, the last blockade by which a man or woman breaks on his way to ruin is the blockade of a good mother's love and a good mother's prayers. When you are a bondslave in Sodom, when doom, final and eternal, seems little short of certain, then it is that tender memories, like delivering angels, lay their hands upon you and lead you out into the high uplands of abiding and saving faith.

But, mark me, the mother who wins pays the price. There are women who seem to resent being women. They complain that the woman has the brunt to bear. That is true. "Now there stood by the Cross of Jesus His mother." That attitude is typical. She is ever by the Cross. That is the reason that her sons and daughters so often are crowned. The woman who refuses to pay, the woman who dodges the cross, also dodges the crown, both for herself and those whom she loves.

The world has changed much since this great woman lived. Life has become far easier in a thousand ways. Travel is easier. Housekeeping is easier. Communication is far easier. And labor-saving devices have been invented by the thousand. Yet with all this, we have found no easy way of mothering our children. We must still grope into the Valley of the Shadow of Death to bring them into life, and when they are here, for them we must daily die. That is what motherhood cost yesterday. That is what it cost my mother. That is what it will cost you. Thank God for the vast company that do not shrink, but count it a privilege to pay the price. Here you are this morning in God's house. A star of hope hangs in your sky. You are rejoicing in the fellowship of a present Savior, and you are looking forward to the good day when you shall find an eternal home and meet with those you have loved long since and lost awhile.

This peace and these blessings are due mainly to your mother. She shunned not the cross. She bled in order that you might be blessed. Therefore you ought to appreciate her. If she is with you today you ought to give her a place in your heart. Her arm-chair ought to have the warmest place by the fireside. You ought to be careful of her, for she has been careful of you. You ought to be patient with her, for she has been patient with you. You ought to mother her, for she has mothered you. You ought to, above all else, respond to the deepest longing of her heart—that is that you should be God's man and God's woman. Oh, I call every man and woman of us here present this morning to a new surrender and to a new loyalty to our Lord, not only for Christ's sake, but for Mother's sake.

XIII

SELF-ENCOURAGEMENT—DAVID

I Samuel 30: 6

"But David encouraged himself in the Lord his God." Of all the benefactors that we meet in this world there are few that render so great a service as the courage bringer. There is no finer art than that of putting heart into people who have become despairful. There is no more splendid service that any of us can possibly render than that of relighting the candle of hope and expectancy in the darkened lives of those about us.

So we are naturally profoundly interested in the hero of our text. We are interested in him because he is an encourager. He is a living antidote to fear. He brings that without which no man can live at his best or render his largest service. If you want to help where help is most needed, learn how to encourage people. If you want to make a contribution to life of high and genuine worth master the secret of changing sobs into songs.

This is a vastly helpful and important service in the first place because a discouraged man is in large measure a defeated and useless man. How many folks fail in the battle of life not for lack of ability, nor from lack of opportunity, nor even from lack of eagerness to succeed, but from lack of courage. That was why the man of one talent failed. He tried to blame his failure upon his master, but his master was not to blame, nor were his circumstances, nor was his ability. He himself was to blame. He was too easily discouraged. He was so soon mastered by fear. And fear and discouragement take the elasticity out of our step, kill our initiative and sap the thews of our strength.

If you are to succeed at any task you must work at it hopefully. That is true in the business world. That is equally true if your fight is with some physical disease. The man who is discouraged in the grip of a physical malady has far less chance to recover than the man who keeps up his courage and refuses to lose heart and hope. That is also true of your moral fight. If you expect to win in the battle for Christlike character, if you expect to lay hold on the crown of real manhood and womanhood, you must not lose heart. You must not allow yourself to become discouraged, for to lose courage is to lose the battle.

Then the work of the encourager is an important work in the second place because discouragement is one of the greatest sources of human wretchedness. How many unhappy people there are! Some of you listening to me are restless and wretched and miserable. Why? Because you are discouraged. And a discouraged heart is a joyless heart. If you are discouraged this morning, there is little brightness in the sunshine for you and there is little beauty in the springtime and there is little of perfume in the flowers and little of music in the song of birds. A genuine case of discouragement is enough to blind us to a million treasures of beauty. It is enough to make us miserable in spite of all the laughter and glad possibilities of a God-ordered world.

Not only does discouragement make us wretched, not only does it rob us of the joy of the Lord which should be our strength, but at times it causes us to throw away life altogether. I looked into the face of a suicide some months ago. It was a pathetic face, and as I looked at it and thought of my own joy in the privilege of living I could not but say, "Why did you throw away the fine treasure of life?" And the answer that came back from those dumb lips and from that tired, hopeless face was this, "I lost heart. I became utterly discouraged." And when a man is thoroughly discouraged life is no longer a blessing. He may not fling it away, but the joy is gone out of it.

The encourager therefore is a man that keeps the song in life and that prevents life from becoming at once burdensome and useless. For this reason we are profoundly interested in David. He puts heart into us. He make us look up and laugh and sing. He makes us believe in the dawn of tomorrow. He helps us to forget our failures and our defeats, to fling away our fears and to lay hold upon hope and the high expectation of victory.

And yet the text does not say he encouraged others, though that is true. What the text says of him is this: "He encouraged himself." And that, I think, is the biggest thing you could say about him because that is absolutely essential to real encouragement of others. It is next to impossible for me to give to my brother a courage that I do not possess myself. It is very hard indeed for me to allay his fear when my own knees are smiting together. It is hard for me to convince him of victory when I myself am a slave to the fear of defeat. It is hard for me to inspire him with the hope of a glad reunion in God's House if my own eyes are turned only to the dust that sleeps in the grave-yard.

He encouraged himself. That is a fine art which is indeed worth learning. It is a great privilege to be encouraged by another. It is wonderful to have a friend who is able to put hope into you when you are hopeless. But sometimes such a friend is wanting. Sometimes we seem to be forgotten. Sometimes we seem left absolutely to ourselves. The truth of the matter is that the great battles, the battles in which we lose or win our souls, are fought alone. Happy is the man who has become in some large measure independent of others and who can encourage himself. David was such a man. There was no friend to encourage him, and so he encouraged himself.

How did he do it? That is a vastly important question. How did this discouraged and endangered man learn the blessed secret of self-encouragement? He encouraged himself. How? He did not do it in the first place by denying or ignoring the difficult situation in which he found himself. There were dangers and perplexities and sorrows confronting him that were very real. He could not truthfully deny their existence. He could not stultify his own intelligence. He could not spit in the face of his own reason. He could not so throw dust in the eyes of common sense as to deny the reality of the perils and sorrows in which he found himself.

Now, I know that we can sometimes help ourselves by looking upon the bright side. Some people seem to seek to see only what is disappointing and discouraging. They have a keen eye only for what makes for despair. They have an ear that is attentive only to the discords of life. They forget to rejoice in life's common mercies and every-day blessings. But I have more hope for this kind of man than for one who shuts his eyes to plain palpable facts simply because they are unpleasant.

Neither did David encourage himself by the thought of his own goodness and greatness. He did not encourage himself by patting himself on the back and telling himself what a splendid fellow he was, how resourceful, how righteous, how saintly. The consciousness that we are right with God, that we have walked in our integrity, is a real consolation. But few of us have sufficient of goodness to be of any great consolation to ourselves in our hours of depression and disappointment and discouragement.

Neither did David encourage himself with the prospect of throwing down his task and running away. Many of us try to encourage ourselves in that way. We have undertaken to do a bit of work. It has not succeeded as we expected. What do we do about it? Instead of making up our minds to put more of energy and effort into it, we make up our minds to quit. We have set ourselves to the high task of being Christians. We stumble and fall. What do we then do? We hide ourselves away in the crowd. We cease to strive. We leave off the struggle. We give it up. We leave our church membership a thousand miles away from us and keep it a profound secret among our friends that we ever belonged to the Church at all. To encourage yourself with the promise of quitting is the encouragement of a coward and cannot but result in the end in utter discouragement.

He encouraged himself. How? Here is the secret: "David encouraged himself in the Lord his God." He brought his difficulties, his sorrows, his failures, his perplexities, into the light of the divine countenance. He laid his hand in the hand of Him of whom it is written, "He shall not fail nor be discouraged." He moved into the nearer presence of Him who is the one abiding source of courage. He was the one sure help for David. He is the one sure help for ourselves. "And now, Lord, what wait I for? My hope is in thee."

And will you notice the circumstances in the midst of which this man encouraged himself? It is easy enough to encourage ourselves when there is nothing wrong. You are ready to say, "Of course David could encourage himself. He was a great man, a great poet, a great soldier. Everything was coming his way. He knew nothing of sorrows like mine and of struggles like mine and of disappointments and discouragements like mine. It is easy enough for a man to encourage himself as he lies upon the velvet cushions on board a summer yacht, but it is altogether different when he is clinging to the splintered masts of a wrecking ship and the storm is on and death is laughing with mocking laughter amidst the torn shreds of the rigging."

But David was not in an easy place. He was face to face with a great failure. The city that he was to defend had been raided and captured and destroyed. He had failed at his task and failure was hard for him to bear just as it is hard for you and me. Yet in the midst of failure he encouraged himself in the Lord his God. And because he brought his failure and defeat into the light of the divine presence, he did not believe even failure was fatal. He came to believe that victory might come out of defeat. And so he encouraged himself in the Lord his God.

Maybe you have failed, and this morning you are depressed and out of heart. You have been defeated and you have come out to God's house with your mind

about made up that you will never try again. Oh, believe me, Jesus Christ has abundance of hope for those
who have failed. He promises that though the cup has
been marred in the making, He will make it again.
When His own disciples had failed Him so miserably
and had slept when they should have watched, when
they had slept when they should have prayed, when
they had thrown away their big opportunity in the
garden—He did not throw them away. But instead,
He said, "Arise, let us be going." And they arose and
encouraged themselves in the Lord their God and went
from failure to success and from defeat to victory.
And so may you go, for whatever yesterday may have
been, you may start anew this morning.

> "Each day is a new beginning,
> Each morn is the world made new;
> Oh, you who are weary of sinning,
> Here's a hope and a chance for you."

Not only was David facing defeat, but he was facing
hatred and unpopularity and loneliness and lack of
appreciation that had come as a result of his failure.
There had been a time when David was in high favor.
Yesterday men applauded him. Yesterday their lips
were full of compliments and they were ready to throw
bouquets at him. Today he is the most unpopular man
in the camp. Nobody seems to love him. Nobody
seems to believe in him. Nobody seems to think that
he is of any account at all.

Now, there are some things harder to bear than that,
I suppose, but there are very few. Some of you to
whom I am speaking know what it means. For months
you have been a stranger in a great city. You have
felt yourself utterly alone, forgotten, neglected. Maybe

you are bleeding from a wound that you cannot reveal
to any human eye. Maybe you are neglected and
scorned by those who should love you best. Maybe you
have got lost in the big crowd and feel that nobody
cares whether you go or come, live or die.

What are you going to do about it? Lock yourself
in with your sorrow and let it poison for you every
fountain of life? Would it not be wiser to take
David's course and if men fail to encourage you, encourage yourself in the Lord your God? Would it not
be wiser to remember that earth has no sorrow that
Jesus Christ cannot heal and cannot sweeten? Do you
remember those pathetic words of our Lord? He had
become vastly unpopular. Men hated Him. The great
crowd deserted Him. Only His disciples clung to Him,
and then one day near the end of the journey He said
to them, "It shall come to pass that you will scatter,
every one to his own and leave me alone."

How did Jesus come to say this? He would never
have said it if He had not dreaded being alone. He
hated loneliness. He hated it with a sensitiveness to
which we are strangers. But He faced that loneliness
without flinching and without fear. Why? "He encouraged himself in the Lord His God." Listen to
what He says, "Ye shall leave me alone. And yet I am
not alone; the Father is with me." And there may
always be that consolation for ourselves. Whatever
hatred and misunderstanding and unpopularity may
come to us, we can find encouragement in the Lord our
God.

Then not only had David become unpopular because
of his failure, but he had come face to face with personal danger. Death was rattling the latch of his door.
The people out yonder who had once idolized him were

threatening to stone him. He was in the midst of peril. He was in a situation where most men's faces would have been blanched with fear. What did he do when he stood eye to eye with danger? He encouraged himself in the Lord his God.

And thank God, that sure refuge is open to every one of us. Countless multitudes of God's saints have so encouraged themselves in the presence of danger and faced it calm and unafraid. David Livingstone tells us how one night sleeping in Africa he heard the wild screams of the savages as they sought him. The instinct of self-preservation seized him and he rose and broke into a wild run into the dark. But he had run only a few steps when he was arrested by a blessed promise from God's Word. And he tells us that he went back and lay down knowing that it was the word of a perfect Gentleman. He encouraged himself in the Lord his God.

Yonder stands a man on board a merchant vessel in the Mediterranean. For fourteen days that ship has been the plaything of the tempest. It has borne up as long as it can and now it is going to pieces, for the storm still rages and its fury is unspent and unwearied. About this man is a ghastly crew, fear-blanched and hunger-pinched. They have eaten nothing for many days. This strange man lays hold upon a broken mast of that wrecking vessel and lifts his voice in a glad shout of encouragement. He cries, "Be of good cheer." What is the secret of his cheer? Listen: "There stood by me this night the angel of God whose I am and whom I serve, saying, Fear not, Paul." In the midst of this awful peril this saintly Jew had been encouraging himself in the Lord his God.

Are you confronted this morning by dangers in whose

presence you feel utterly powerless and hopeless? Are you afraid and panic-stricken in the presence of the demands that are made upon you? There is a source of encouragement that is absolutely sure and unfailing. You may encourage yourself in the Lord your God. That was the secret of the strength of Stephen as he faced the stones. That was the secret of the joyous confidence of the early Apostles in the presence of the threats of their enraged enemies. They encouraged themselves in the Lord their God. And as they went forth in the power of that encouragement men saw their boldness and took knowledge of them that they had been with Jesus.

David was also face to face with personal loss. His own loved ones had been in this destroyed city and now they were gone. It seemed that he would never see them again. There were children missing that he loved even as you love your own. And what did this great man do in the presence of the grim fact of loss and of separation from those that were dear to him? "He encouraged himself in the Lord his God."

There are many here this morning who have suffered loss. While I am speaking, your thoughts turn to widely scattered graves. Some of them are pathetically new and some are older and have grown green under the kiss of the springtime. But we have not forgotten and we can never forget. What will we do in the presence of the grim fact of death? Your little baby toddled right out of your arms and right out of your house one sad day. You have a high chair in which nobody sits and toys with which nobody plays. What will you do about it? Ah, you may do this, if you will—you may encourage yourself in the Lord your God. David did that on this occasion. He did it again years later at

the death of his little boy. He declared with a faith
not even surpassed in the glorious noon-tide of the New
Testament, "I can go to him, but he cannot return to
me." Oh, grief-stricken heart, encourage yourself this
morning in the Lord your God. Let these words drop
afresh like healing balm into your wounded soul.

"Let not your heart be troubled: ye believe in God believe
also in me.
"In my Father's house are many mansions: if it were not
so I would have told you. I go to prepare a place for you.
"And if I go and prepare a place for you, I will come
again, and receive you unto myself; that where I am, there
ye may be also."

This is our consolation and our hope. It is a hope
steadfast and sure. And as the clods cover the faces of
those we love we will not be afraid. We will encourage ourselves in the Lord our God, knowing that
His Word is sure, that one day we shall find those that
we "have loved long since and lost awhile."

This then is the message that I wish to bring to you
this morning, that in whatever circumstances you may
find yourself, all that is needed for your encouragement is here. I know we feel many times like the big
need is for us to get away. Our big longing is to give
up the fight and throw down the burden and hide ourselves from the discouragement and the bitterness of it
all. But let me repeat, all that you need is here, for
God is here and you may find an unfailing source of
joy and encouragement in Him.

You remember how this poet king felt at another
time. A great sorrow was upon him and he longed
for dove's wings that he might find consolation in flight.
But consolation, as he himself learned, does not come

that way. If we find it at all, the consolation that abides, the encouragement that never wanes into discouragement, we must find it in Jesus Christ our Lord. "Cast thy burden upon the Lord and He will sustain thee. He will never suffer the righteous to be moved." May this my text be true of you today. "He encouraged himself in the Lord his God."

XIV

A MURDERER'S PRAYER—DAVID

Psalms 51

"Have mercy upon me, O God." This prayer comes from the lips of a man whose hands are hideous with filth and whose garments are streaked with murder. David, the man after God's own heart, has lost God. He has committed crime. He has committed a double crime. He has wrecked the home of a faithful and a loyal soldier. He has not only wrecked his home, but he has taken his life as well. How this sin of adultery sprang upon David like a wild beast, we know. How it led him on to the yet greater sin of murder, that we also know.

When did this great fall come to David? When was it that this man after God's own heart lost his grip of his Lord. When was it that he forsook the Good Shepherd? When was it that he became guilty first of the evil thought, the unholy desire, then adultery, then murder? David did not fall in the days of his adversity. He did not fall in the stress and strain of conflict. He did not fall when he was winning his crown. He fell after he had won it.

Now days of conflict are not without danger, but you will agree with me that they are not our most dangerous days. The young fellow who is having a hard time trying to establish himself in business or in his profession, he is not the one who is subjected to the most

savage temptations. He is not the one for whom we
are most afraid. The days of our danger are the days
when we have arrived. For one that can stand success
and keep sweet and pure and Christlike, there are a
hundred that can stand failure. David had succeeded.

In the second place, David was idle. His had been
a busy life. There had been much fighting in it. There
had been much of stir and of movement. He had found
it necessary to hide in the caves and in the mountains.
As he had hidden there even in those busy moments he
had sung songs that will outlast the centuries. He
interwove the snarls and the growls of the mountain
lions in his marvelous poetry as he said, "The young
lions do lack and suffer hunger, but they that seek the
Lord shall not want any good."

But today he is idle. Today he has nothing to do.
And no man can stand the strain of idleness for any
long time. That time-worn saying that "the idle brain
is the devil's work shop" is everlastingly true. When
is it that most of our young people go wrong? It is
not in the hours of the rush of business. It is in the
hours of leisure. It is in the hours when there is nothing to do. Nature abhors a vacuum, and unless we
overcome evil with good we are going to overcome good
with evil.

Then David had reached that trying period of middle
life. Youth has its dangers that are very genuine. Old
age also has its dangers. But more people go wrong
and more people fail morally between the ages of forty
and fifty, I think, than in any other decade. It is an
age when we have lost something of the fine idealism
of our early years. We have stopped giving any attention to the pansies, as one has said, and are devoting
all our time to the potatoes. We have not yet come

within the gleam of the lights of home. We are too far from spring to have our ideals. We are too far from rest of eventide to be solemnized by the thoughts of the homegoing. We need prayer and watchfulness at all times. But we need now especially to pray this prayer: "Lord, revive thy work in the midst of the years." The most marvelous story in the Book of Acts is the one that closes with this victorious sentence: "For the man was above forty years old upon whom this miracle of healing showed."

It was, then, this successful and victorious and prosperous and idle middle-aged king who fell. His temptation was first only a forbidden look, only an evil thought. But the thought grew into an act, and the King found himself that most dastardly of scoundrels, a home-wrecker. But there might have been the least extenuating bit of circumstance about this terrible crime. It was committed in the heat of passion. But the crime that followed, the murder of the loyal and faithful man whom he had so deeply wronged, that crime was committed deliberately and in cold blood. I know of no murder in history that surpasses it for blackness.

Of course David never dreamed that his sin would go that far. Only an evil thought at one end, but murder at the other. When the devil gets us on his toboggan slide there is no telling where we are going to stop. Clarence V. T. Richardson began in his early ministry with innocent flirtations with girls of his congregation. He ended with the murder of a girl he had wronged, and a seat in the electric chair. Sin has tremendous growing power.

But strange as it may seem, this kingly man, once close to God, has become a murderer, a murderer without one single extenuating circumstance. If there was ever a crime for which there was no slightest excuse it is his crime. And yet, wonder of all wonders and miracle of all miracles, this man David found his way back into the divine favor, and has succeeded, by the grace of God, in being a great blessing to the world.

What is the secret? If I learn the way that he took to get from the Far Country into his Father's House, maybe my sinful feet might walk it. For of this I am sure, that David stands in no greater need of forgiveness than I do. He is no more needy than you. How did David find God?

The first step in David's salvation was that God in His mercy sent him a preacher. Account for it how you may, it has pleased God by the foolishness of preaching to save them that believe. This preacher took his life in his hands when he went to call on David that day. A lion-hearted preacher was Nathan, and he was skillful as he was brave. He told David a very stirring story of the injustice of one man against another. He told of how a man with great herds stole the one lamb of the poor man. And David clenched his fists and bit his lips and said, "The man that did that thing shall surely die."

Oh, it is so much easier to get us to rage against the other man's sin than to be indignant against our own. David listened to this sermon and never took a word of it to himself. He said, "This man Nathan is certainly digging up that scoundrel that has been sheep stealing, whoever he is." And then Nathan did a tremendously courageous thing. He put his finger into the face of this lust-smeared and blood-stained king and said, "Thou art the man."

Then what happened? Many a man in David's position would have killed the preacher. That is what Herod did. But David's cheeks went white and his knees went weak and he fell on his face and sobbed out his prayer. It was a prayer that was altogether becoming the lips of one who had sinned as he had sinned. It was just the prayer for the murderer. That is not all. It was a prayer for just such sinners as ourselves.

"Have mercy upon me, O God, according to thy loving kindness: according unto the multitude of thy tender mercies blot out my transgressions.

"Wash me thoroughly from mine iniquity, and cleanse me from my sin.

"Create in me a clean heart, O God; and renew a right spirit within me.

"Cast me not away from thy presence; and take not thy holy spirit from me.

"Restore unto me the joy of thy salvation; and uphold me with thy free spirit.

"Then will I teach transgressors thy ways; and sinners shall be converted unto thee."

Yes, David prayed. The King with voice choked with sobs made his humble confession to almighty God. And what he said as he fell in His presence was that universal confession: "I have sinned." Over and over again he speaks of his sin as his own, as "my sin," "my iniquity," "my transgression." He offers no excuse. He pleads no mitigating circumstance. He lays the blame on no other shoulders.

Now, there is real penitence here. But as long as we confess our sins and then excuse them there is no hope for us. A man came into my study the other day and confessed his sins with tears. I prayed with him and then he prayed. And he went away. But I have but little hope of that man. Why? Oh, he confessed that he had been a great sinner, but he laid the blame for the fact on somebody else. Now, brother, do you not see that as long as there is an excuse for your sin you are not guilty? As long as somebody else is to blame for what you do then you are blameless. To come with excuses before God with a stain upon your heart is to go away as stained as you came with the added stain of hypocrisy. There is no excuse for sin. May God help us to know it. Therefore come with this heart cry upon your lips, for it belongs to the best of men and it belongs to the worst of men, "I have sinned."

Not only does David acknowledge his sin, but with conscience illuminated by the Holy Spirit he sees his sin as an act of rebellion against God. "Against thee, thee only have I sinned." That sounds strange. He had sinned against Uriah. He had sinned against the wife of Uriah. He had sinned against the children in his home. He had sinned against his kingdom. He had sinned against society, but all this was as nothing in comparison with the awful blow he had struck at the infinite Father who loved him.

Sin wrongs everybody, but it shoots its sharpest shaft into the heart of Jesus Christ. All who love you may be wounded by your sin, but the one who is most deeply wounded is the One who loves you best. The sufferings of Jesus Christ were not ended on Calvary. Day by day He is being wounded by those who sin against His love, and every act of wrongdoing is an act of outlawry against God. And every transgression wounds the heart of God. Oh, that we might see it and fall before Him, as David fell, and say, "I have sinned against thee, against thee only have I sinned."

And having made his confession, for what is this blood-stained and guilty man making request? For what does he ask? Listen: "Have mercy upon me." Oh, that is your prayer and that is mine. That is the prayer for every one of us. "Have mercy upon me." Mercy is kindness to the undeserving. David did not ask for justice. I am not going to ask for that. He smote upon his breast like the poor publican and said, "God, be merciful to me a sinner."

And the measure of God's mercy! What is it? How much mercy does David ask? He does not say, "Have mercy upon me according to my sincerity." He did not count much on his own sincerity. He does not say, "Have mercy upon me according to my rank, according to my position." These, too, went for nothing. He does not say, "Have mercy upon me according to my genius, according to my vast ability." He does not even say, "Have mercy upon me according to the depth of my earnestness and the bitterness of my tears." But this was his prayer: "Have mercy upon me, O God, according to thy loving kindness." Oh, that is the request that he needed to make. It is a petition that is suited to all of us. This is true because it is a prayer for infinite mercy.

And will you see what is the content of that mercy? In what is the mercy of God to consist? It is to consist, first of all, in forgiveness. "Wash me," he cries, "and I shall be whiter than snow." David is so tired of being unclean. He is so weary of being soiled and filthy and unholy. He said, "Lord, make me clean once more. I know my sins are as scarlet, but if thou dost wash me I shall be whiter than snow."

And not only does he ask for cleansing, but he asks

172 MORE SERMONS ON BIBLICAL CHARACTERS

for a new heart. He wants a new nature. He realizes that he is not only a sinner, but that he is sinful. And so he said, "Create in me a clean heart, O God."

> "Thy nature, gracious Lord, impart,
> Come quickly from above.
> Write thy new name upon my heart,
> Thy new best name of love."

He yearns that God may take away out of his bosom the heart of stone and give him a heart of flesh. He wants to be born again, born from above, born with the spirit of lust dethroned and with the Spirit of God enthroned. And so he said, "Create within me a clean heart."

And this man is not seeking these blessings simply that he may escape hell. I do not think there is the least element of the fear of punishment in this prayer. I believe the thought of punishment would have been rather welcome to a man who was suffering as David was suffering. He would have felt as if it might have eased his conscience a bit. He is not afraid of being punished. But he is afraid of that uncleanliness that is robbing him of the presence of God. And in this prayer he is crying like a lost child after the father that he has wronged and driven from his presence. He feels that life itself would be hell without the divine presence. And so he is clinging to God's skirts and saying, "Cast me not away from thy presence. Lord, do not throw me away. Do not cast me off utterly. I know I deserve it, but my heart crieth out after thee. As the hart panteth after the water brooks, so panteth my soul after thee, O God."

And then he seems to gather courage, and he reminds the Lord of the old days in which he knew Him, of

the old intimacies and the old fellowships of yesterday. And he sobs out one more petition: "Restore unto
me the joy of thy salvation. Lord, give me back the
lost song. Give me back the radiant face. My tears
have been my meat day and night. My sin is ever
before me. The whole world has looked red to me since
that terrible crime. Let me know the old joy that will
be so blessedly new. Give me back the light of thy
countenance. Grant, O Lord, that the lame may again
leap as a hart and the tongue of the dumb burst forth
once more into song."

I wonder if I am not talking to men and women tonight that once knew God but have lost Him. It may
not have been through some great and glaring sin like
that of David. The chances are altogether against that.
Most of us do not sin in that hideous way. You have
lost Him maybe simply through neglect of duty,
through carelessness or through the tug and pressure
of the world. But tonight His face is hidden from you
and the once blessed experience is only a memory. Oh,
will you not join with me in the prayer of this
blood-guilty man, "Restore unto me the joy of thy
salvation"?

And last of all, this man sobs out his vow of conse-
cration. He said, "Lord, if thou wilt take me back
again, if thou wilt wash me and restore me once more
to thy favor, I will tell the story of thy redeeming
grace. I will let the world know that thou delightest in
mercy and that with thee is plenteous redemption. Restore unto me the joy of thy salvation and uphold me
with thy free spirit. Then will I teach transgressors
thy ways and sinners shall be converted unto thee."

Certainly he ought to be willing to do that. Certainly any man ought to be willing. How often we

want to be healed and then are ashamed of the physician. O heart, God is calling us always. He is saying, "Go home to thy friends and tell how great things the Lord hath done for thee, and hath had compassion on thee."

And what was the outcome of this man's prayer? You know. God heard it and saved him. "I have sinned." And the answer came: "And the Lord hath put away thy sin." It is a blessed truth. It is as true today as it was in that far-off yesterday. "For if we confess our sins He is faithful and just to forgive us our sins and to cleanse us from all unrighteousness."

And this murderer rises from his knees, and his tears of penitence have been kissed into jewels. And he is true to his vows. He does teach transgressors the ways of God. And the lilt of his song rings down the centuries. "Blessed is the man whose transgression is forgiven, whose sin is covered. Blessed is the man unto whom the Lord imputeth not iniquity. Rejoice in the Lord, ye righteous, and shout thy joy, all ye that are upright in heart."

Yes, he sings as he rises from his knees. And he sings as he continues the journey of his life. And he goes down into the valley with a song. And he walks into the waters of death with the lilt of his music still ringing in the air. We lean across the years and hear him tonight. The music floats to us sweet as that which rang above the Judean hills.

"The Lord is my shepherd; I shall not want.

"He maketh me to lie down in green pastures: he leadeth me beside the still waters.

"He restoreth my soul: he leadeth me in the paths of righteousness for his name's sake.

"Yea, though I walk through the valley of the shadow of

death, I will fear no evil: for thou art with me; thy rod and
thy staff they comfort me.

"Thou preparest a table before me in the presence of mine
enemies: thou anointest my head with oil; my cup runneth
over.

"Surely goodness and mercy shall follow me all the days
of my life: and I will dwell in the house of the Lord forever."

When I remember that this was the song of a murderer I thank God and take courage and believe that
there is hope and pardon even for me. That though my
sins are as scarlet and my life streaked and soiled with
many transgressions I may yet be made every whit
whole. And when my sense of sin tends to make me
dumb in His presence I shall dare to pour out before
Him the prayer of this murderer, "Have mercy upon
me, O God, according to thy loving kindness."

XV

THE STARVATION COMMITTEE—THE FOUR LEPERS

II Kings 7 : 3

"Why sit we here until we die?" This is the wise question that was propounded by the members of a certain committee that met a great many years ago. The place of meeting is the gate of the city of Samaria. Samaria is being besieged by the army of Syria. For many days it has been closely shut in. The food supply has been cut off. Hunger is stalking its streets. Unless relief soon comes many will die. Among the first to feel the pinch of hunger were the members of this starvation committee. They were beggars to begin with. A calamity that brought privation to those in better circumstances would soon mean utter starvation to themselves. So they are dying by the inch now, these four leprous beggars. And it is to cope with their trying situation that this committee meeting is called.

Now the personnel of this starvation committee is very interesting. Its interest, however, does not lie in the fact that these men were members of the aristocracy. They are not conspicuous for either their rank or wealth. Every man of them is a leper. Every man is penniless. Every man is being tortured by hunger. Every man is fisticuffing with ghastly death. But we are interested in these men because of their fine common sense. Through their deliberations they came to the wisest possible conclusions.

176

The first conclusion to which this committee comes is this—they resolved upon some kind of action. "Resolved that we now act, for why sit we here until we die?" It is a good day for any committee, it is a good day for any member of any committee when such a decision is reached. It is so hard to get action. It is so easy for us just to sit and sit and deliberate and deliberate and talk and talk and never do anything.

The reason, I think, that this committee avoided such a disaster was the fact that they were being driven to action by the pressure of great and compelling needs. If all your needs are met it is very easy for you to defer doing anything. If you have no heartache, if you have no burning thirst, if you have no gnawing hunger, then I am not at all surprised that you do nothing. Christian can remain very quietly at home in the City of Destruction till he becomes conscious of a terrible burden that is crushing him down. But having realized this, inactivity is no longer possible. He must needs put his fingers into his ears and rush away even from the loved ones that would detain him, crying "Life, life, eternal life!"

The second reason that led these wise men to resolve upon action was that they knew that almost any action is better than inaction. They realized that it is better to make a thousand blunders and to suffer a thousand defeats than to refuse to battle. They knew that it is far better to fall down again and again than to be too cowardly to ever really stand upon your feet. They considered that of all failures, the supreme failure was to be so afraid of failing that you do nothing at all.

They knew then, these wise men, that there was absolutely nothing to be gained by inaction. "Suppose we simply sit still," one might have suggested. "If we

178 MORE SERMONS ON BIBLICAL CHARACTERS

do," came the quick and intelligent reply, "we will gain nothing. We will surely die, that is all. It is needless for us to wait for something to turn up. It is needless for us to lie down here in the gate of this city with the expectation that somebody will bring us a pitcher of milk and a loaf of bread during the night while we sleep. Waiting will not get us anywhere. It never has. It never will. We can keep on waiting if we make up our minds to it, but the one sure reward of our waiting will not be food. It will not be satisfaction for our hunger. It will be death and death only. Therefore, why sit we here until we die? Inaction means certain death. Therefore let us act. Let us do something."

And now I bring to you an old question: "How shall we escape if we neglect so great salvation?" Mark you, the question is not, How shall we escape if we fight against God? It is not, How shall we escape if we seek to destroy the Church? It is not, How shall we escape if we burn up our Bibles? It is not, How shall we escape if we become drunkards, bootleggers or gamblers? It is not, How shall we escape if we become adulterers or murderers? The question is this: "How shall we escape if we neglect so great salvation?" How shall we escape if we let the salvation that is offered to us in Christ Jesus alone?

And what is the answer to that question? There is but one possible answer to it. There is no escape. To refuse to accept salvation is to miss being saved. To refuse to know Jesus Christ as a personal Savior is simply to miss the privilege of knowing Him. How shall I escape if I let my food alone? Answer—I shall not escape. How did Mayor MacSwiney escape when he refused to eat? He did not escape. He died. And the reason he died was not because he destroyed the food supply of Ireland and England. The reason he died was because he neglected to eat. And so shall you die spiritually and die eternally if you refuse Jesus Christ, who alone is the Bread of Life and the Water of Life.

How shall I escape if I neglect all means of mental development? The answer again is just this: There is no escape. I will simply remain illiterate and ignorant. It is not necessary that I destroy the school buildings of the land. It is not necessary that I burn down all the public libraries. It is not necessary that I mutilate the books. All that is necessary is just this—that I simply let them alone. If I am to reach my highest mental development I must make an effort to do so. But to continue uncultured and ignorant all that is necessary is that I do nothing at all.

It may be that I am speaking to some who are not musicians. Yet you may love music. But how did you come to fail to be a musician? The reason you are not a master is not due to the fact that you have been a wrecker of violins and of musical instruments in general. It is not because you have been a murderer of musicians. I do not say for a moment, however, that there have not been times when you have felt like doing so. When, for instance, you have heard a solo without either words or tune, or have witnessed a song turned into a kind of trapeze for the performing of vocal stunts. Then you may have felt that murder would have been a gratifying procedure. But after all, that does not account for your ignorance of music. You are ignorant because you have simply neglected music.

The truth of the matter is that you do not expect to be proficient in literature, you do not expect to be proficient in music, in baseball, in tennis, or even in mumblepeg by simply letting them alone. You do not expect to acquire skill in anything by the neglect of that particular thing. And yet such is our folly in matters of religion that we sometimes seem to fancy that we can be Christians by simply ignoring Christ. We seem to hope that we can reap the benefits of the death and resurrection of our Lord by simply sitting idly by and acting as if the Bible were only a myth and the supreme truths of revelation nothing more than cunningly devised fables. Oh, I commend to you the good sense of this starvation committee. Its members resolved that at least they would do something.

> "He made no mistakes, took no wrong road.
> He never fumbled the ball.
> He never went down 'neath the weight of a load—
> He simply did nothing at all.
>
> "He lost no hard fight in defense of the right.
> Never bled with his back to the wall.
> He never fell faint in his climb to the light—
> He simply did nothing at all.
>
> "So death came nigh, for life slipped by,
> And he feared for the Judgment Hall;
> When they asked him why, he said with a sigh,
> 'I simply did nothing at all.'
>
> "Oh, God will pardon your blunder, my friend,
> Or regard with pity your fall;
> But the one big sell that surely means hell
> Is to simply do nothing at all."

Now, having resolved on action the next question to decide was what they would do. There were two roads open to them, seeing that they had determined to move.

One of these roads led into the city. "Suppose we go into the city," said one. "No," was the reply. "We have been in the city. We cannot obtain bread there. Death is an absolute certainty if we go back into the city of Samaria." So you see that they have two certainties before them, certain death to stay where they are, certain death if they go into the city. Then one offers a second resolution. "Resolved that we fall into the hands of the Syrians."

Certainly the man who offered that resolution produced a bit of a sensation. The starving men about him gasp. "Resolved that we go out and actually put ourselves into the hands of the enemy!" At first they looked at the mover of that resolution as if they thought him absolutely mad. But they changed their minds as he began to speak to his motion. Listen to him. Possibly he spoke somewhat after this fashion.

"Gentlemen, I am not asking you to join me in an expedition to the camp of the Syrians because I think we can force them to give us bread. There are tens of thousands of them and they are armed and we are only unarmed beggars. Nor am I asking you to go because these Syrians are our friends. They are not our friends. They are our enemies. Nor am I asking you to go because they have invited us and promised to feed us if we go. They have done nothing of the kind. Nor am I basing my plea on the fact that others have gone to their camp and have been helped. They have not fed one single man of us so far as I know. My one big reason for offering this seemingly mad resolution is this: It is not absolutely certain that they will kill us if we go. There is, of course, every probability that they will. The chances are a thousand to one against us. Yet there is that one chance. It seems to me sensible to take that chance, for to remain here or to go into the city is certain death."

Now this man was truly wise. He is worth listening to. "Here we stand," says he, "at the forks of the road. If we remain here we will die. Two roads stretch away from us, one into the city and the other to the camp of the Syrians. If we take the road to the city we know what we will find. We are absolutely sure of it. We will find death. If we take the road that leads to the camp of the Syrians we will probably find death. Yet death is not an absolute certainty. Therefore, I move that we fall into the hands of the Syrians."

The resolution was put and carried unanimously. And at once they rose, though it was now twilight, and put their resolution into action. That is fine. If a good resolution comes to you, act on it at once. These men turned their faces toward the enemy. They do not go eagerly as men who have great expectations. They know that there is every chance that they will be killed. They know that at any moment as they come near the camp they are likely to be challenged. They know that at any moment they are likely to be struck down. And yet they go knowing that there is nothing to be lost by going. If they are killed their fate will be no worse than they would have met if they had stayed where they were.

Now they are very near the camp. They have become exceedingly cautious. They crouch upon their sore knees. Every instant they are expecting to hear one shout, "Halt! Who goes there?" Every moment they are looking to feel the prick of a spear or the thrust of a sword. But there is no challenge and no enemy springs upon them. In fact there is not a man in sight. This is true though they are now within a very few feet of the first tent. They crawl cautiously nearer till they are able to touch the tent with their hands. Is it life that is on the inside or is it death? They do not know. Then full of fear one slightly lifts a fold of the tent and peeps within. Not a soul is there. They gather courage and enter.

And what a glad surprise is theirs. Instead of finding a deadly enemy they find something else that brings to them unutterable joy. They find an abundant supply of food. They fall to and eat with the greediness of starving men, fruits and bread and cheese and old Syrian wine. And when they have eaten all in the first tent they creep to the next and eat again until at last they can eat no more. And then they begin to gather up the treasures of silver and gold and costly garments and hide them. And after they have enriched themselves and after they have fully satisfied their hunger, they find that enough remains for tens of thousands just as poverty stricken and just as hunger pinched as they themselves were.

So you see that in taking their one flimsy chance they found everything for which their hearts yearned. Why do you not act with something of their wisdom? You are not asked to trust yourself to an enemy. You are asked to trust yourself to a Friend. The One to whom I am calling you is One who loves you with an everlasting love. He is One who has come to seek and to save that which is lost. He is come to seek you for love's sake. "For God so loved the world that he gave his only begotten Son, that whosoever believeth in him should not perish, but have everlasting life."

Then your case is unlike that of the lepers because you are invited. "Come, for all things are now ready."

You are expected. You are waited for at the King's court. A banquet has been prepared for you at an infinite price. Your Lord and Master has sent me to you with this wooing word upon my lips: "Come." Over and over again it is repeated throughout the Word. "Come unto me all that labor and are heavy laden, and I will give you rest." You are invited. Your welcome is sure. "For him that cometh unto me I will in no wise cast out."

And if the word of our Lord needed any proof we have the testimony of an innumerable company that no man can number. No doubt you have met those who are members of the Church in whose experience you did not believe. But, thank God, you have met the other kind, too. You have seen those and have been privileged to know those who have been wonderfully transformed and remade by the power of God. And these today are ready to declare with a conviction that we cannot resist that "He is able to save unto the uttermost them that come unto God by Him." They show by the peace and power and richness of their lives that it is true that "He satisfieth the longing soul."

But maybe some of you do not feel quite sure. You may be saying this: "Suppose I go down front and surrender to Christ the best I know and enter the Church and seek to become a faithful follower of the Lord, would it get me anywhere? Will I come to know Christ for myself? I am not sure that I would." Well, assuming that you are not sure and assuming that the testimony of all who have tried Him and found Him true is worth nothing, this at least remains: You know that you are not going to get anywhere doing as you have been doing. You know that your inaction will

never bring you into the blessed fellowship of Jesus
Christ. You certainly will never find salvation by refusing to take it. Since this is true, suppose you try
the other way. To travel the same road you have been
traveling means death. At least death is not a certainty if you make an effort to know Jesus. So then
have the good sense to give yourself the advantage of
the doubt.

Suppose you do come, suppose you make an honest
effort to be a Christian and suppose, though it is a
thing that never happened, you do not get anywhere
at all. Have you lost anything? Are you any the
worse off? If the Prodigal Son leaves the company of
the swine in the Far Country and comes home, even if
he is not welcome he is no worse off. If he is still
allowed to be hungry at the Father's house that is no
worse fate than was his in the Far Country. And if
no rich garment is given him, remember that he had
only beggars' rags where he was.

I suppose that is what the Prodigal thought when he
turned his face toward home. He did not seem to
expect much. He thought maybe by humbling himself
and begging he could get a place in the servants' quar-
ters. "I have sinned against Heaven and in thy sight
and am no more worthy to be called thy son. Make me
as one of thy hired servants." That was the speech
he had made up his mind to make. But think of the
glory of his surprise. "When he was yet a great way
off his father saw him and ran and fell on his neck and
kissed him." And when the lad began to make his
abject speech his father broke in on it and said, "Bring
forth the best robe and put it on him and put a ring
on his hand and shoes on his feet. And bring hither

the fatted calf and kill it and let us eat and be merry."
Oh, there is a glorious surprise for you if you will
only come to your Lord.

But there is something else very fine about this committee. They had a second meeting after they had
eaten their fill and had enriched themselves. "Then
they said one to another, We do not well. This day is
a day of good tidings, and we hold our peace; if we
tarry till the morning some mischief will come upon
us: now therefore come, that we may go and tell the
king's household." Oh, great committee! Great-
hearted lepers! They said, "Our conduct in this matter
is mighty shabby. We are altogether unworthy of the
great blessings that have come to us. Here is more
than we could use in a thousand lifetimes and there are
multitudes that are starving yonder in the city. What
ingrates we are for not hurrying away and carrying
the good news to them, for this is a day of good tidings."

Not only did they decide to tell the good news to
others, but they decided to tell that good news at once.
They said, "If we wait till the morning light some
calamity will befall us. We have a wonderful story to
tell. We will not postpone the telling of it till our
friends yonder in the city have starved to death. We
will go at once. The news we have is blessed news.
The needs we are seeking to meet are very pressing
needs. We will tell it and we will tell it now."

Oh, come, you members of the Church who know
the Lord, and sit at the feet of these leprous beggars.
The Lord give us grace to learn from them. You have
heard of the Bread of Life. You claim to be feasting
on that Bread for yourself. You have heard of the
Water of Life. You claim to have kissed that brim-
ming and abiding spring with your own parched lips.

Are your high claims true? If so, how can you sit still? How can you remain silent? This, my brethren, is a day of good tidings. We have the most wonderful story ever told. May the Lord give us grace to tell it.

Then, too, we must realize that this is a needy world. The people of Samaria were no more starving for physical bread on that day than our friends and our loved ones are starving for the Bread of Life. I read some time ago of a man who shot himself in one of our great cities. He left a letter recounting the terrible sorrows through which he had passed, his hard fight against despair. Then he added: "All these dark dreary days I have been hoping that some man would ask me to become a Christian." Oh, the sin and the need and the hunger of heart! Go to these needy men with your message. Go now. If you tarry some evil will come upon you. It will be the evil of a guilty conscience and a lost sense of the divine presence.

But to you who have never surrendered your lives to Christ I make this appeal, I bring this question: Why sit you here until you die? What hope have you for salvation apart from Jesus Christ? Do you not know that "there is none other name under heaven given among men whereby you must be saved"? Do you not realize that if you are ever saved you must act? Do you not know that if you ever possess you must take? Are you not conscious of the fact that if Jesus Christ ever enters into your life you must of your own choice let Him in? "Behold I stand at the door and knock. If any man will hear my voice and will open the door I will come in and sup with him and he with me." But you must open the door. Will you not open it tonight? Why sit you here until you die?

A few years ago I was conducting a service for children and young people. I held up a piece of money and said, "I will give this piece of money to any one who was fifteen years of age his last birthday. Who will come and get it?" But one fifteen-year-old looked at another and nobody moved. I then dropped to fourteen, then to thirteen, then to twelve, then eleven. But nobody moved. I saw one lad sitting on the edge of his seat ready for the spring. I did not know his age, but I knew when the time came he was going to take me at my word. I called for ten, and nine and the word was hardly out of my mouth till he came and claimed the money.

The next day after this service a woebegone lad came to me and said: "Brother Chappell, when are you going to give away some more money?" I said, "Let me ask you a question. How old are you?" "Twelve," was the reply. "Why did you not get that which I gave away yesterday?" Why did he not? It was not because he ran from the room when I made the proposition. It was not because he swore at me and threw a book at me. How did he miss it? He simply let it alone. So you may miss all the fine prizes of life. So you may miss the supreme prize, the privilege of knowing and loving and serving Jesus Christ. Why will you do it? Answer this question: Why sit you here until you die?

THE UNDYING FIRE—MOSES

Exodus 3 : 2

"And the Angel of the Lord appeared unto him in a flame of fire out of the midst of a bush: and he looked, and behold, the bush burned with fire, and the bush was not consumed." This is a marvelous story. One morning an old man set out to his usual task of taking care of a flock of sheep. And the very next morning that same man set out to become the leader and builder of a nation. How was this great change brought about? How was this modest shepherd induced to give up his quiet pastoral life for the feverish life of a great leader? How was this silent dweller of the desert made into a lawgiver and a prophet, both for his own race and for the world?

There is but one adequate answer to this question. That answer is found in the text. "And the Angel of the Lord appeared unto him." But for this experience I am confident that the Moses we know had never existed. But for this experience it is altogether probable that the greatest character in the Old Testament would have passed to his reward without having filled any larger place in the world than that of sheep keeper for a Midianitish priest.

There are many reasons that lead us to the conviction that Moses the shepherd would have continued to be a shepherd to the end of the chapter. First he was

now an old man. He was eighty years of age. Men
do not work revolutions as a rule at that age. No more
do they experience revolutions. "Can a man be born
again when he is old?" It is possible, but it is highly
improbable. If we do not find our Lord and find our
place in His kingdom in the springtime of life the
chances are that we will never find it.

Then Moses had made an effort at this work of free-
ing Israel and had failed. His had been a very disappointing experience. To liberate Israel had been one
of the dreams of his life. It had been breathed into
his heart in his early childhood. It had been with him
during the course of his training at the royal university. His big life purpose, once he had come to the
throne, was to set his people free.

One day he had gone to visit them. There he had
seen the tragedy of slavery eye to eye. An Egyptian
taskmaster was maltreating a certain Hebrew slave.
Moses lost his temper. "His soul leaped to its feet
fire-eyed and defiant." In his hot anger he struck
the offender dead. He then dug a shallow grave,
tumbled his victim into it, covered him with sand and
went back to the palace.

As he turned away from this scene he was upheld by
a twofold conviction. First, he believed that the blow
that he struck was just. He thought that he had taken
his first step towards the emancipation of his people.
Second, he counted upon the loyalty of those for whom
he had struck the blow. No Egyptian had been by
when the deed was done. He counted therefore upon
its being kept secret, since he was sure that the
Israelites would not betray their leader who was ven-
turing so much in their behalf.

But a second visit changed all this. On this occasion

he saw two Hebrews in a hot contention. Again he
interfered. He urged them to desist on the ground
that they were brothers. But his interference was not
welcomed. Instead, one of the parties to the conflict
turned upon him and said with biting sarcasm: "Who
made you a prince and a judge over us? Do you mean
to kill me as you killed the Egyptian?"

This contemptuous question was a revelation to
Moses. It told him of certain facts. It struck his
hopes dead. It was a revelation, first of all, of the
fact that his leadership was not acknowledged nor accepted. In the second place it let him know that the
blow that he had struck in their defense was not in the
least appreciated. His effort had not wakened the
slightest loyalty in those for whom it was made. In
the third place it was a revelation of the fact that
these Hebrew people would not do to depend upon.
He discovered that they were not only physical but
moral slaves. Their fetters were not only around their
limbs, but around their souls as well. He had every
reason to believe that this miserable knave who had
just asked him this question would betray him to the
first Egyptian taskmaster that came along.

What was he to do under these trying circumstances?
There was but one thing to do as he considered the
matter, and that was to leave the country. So he had
left Egypt. He turned away from the greatest kingdom in the world when he had his foot upon the very
steps of the throne. He buried himself in the Midian
desert. After such an experience it was little likely
that he would ever undertake the task again.

Besides all this, Moses was now very pleasantly sit-
uated. His first years in this country of Midian were
very trying and bitter years. He brooded over his loss

and his fruitless sacrifice. He brooded over the hopeless plight of his people. He suffered in his own loneliness. The name of his firstborn signifies this. He called him a name whose meaning is: "I have been a stranger in a strange land."

But these earlier and bitter years have long dropped into the past. Moses has now been here for forty years. He is comfortably married. He has not gone into business for himself. He is looking after the flocks of his wealthy father-in-law. By and by the old man will pass out and his son-in-law will have nothing to do but to step into his shoes and inherit his property. Yes, Moses was, as we say, well fixed.

And that, my brethren, constitutes a great difficulty. How rare it is to see a young man of wealth enter the ministry. How exceedingly rare to find a young girl from the home of a millionaire preparing for the foreign field. God seems almost shut up to the poor for the choice of those who are to do special Christian work.

I know a young man, gifted and well-trained. In his youthful and more enthusiastic days he volunteered for the ministry. He clung to that resolution for some years. He even passed through one of our theological seminaries. But he will never preach. He has too much money. And he still further lessened his chances by marrying a woman of wealth. Money is a great handicap in entering the ministry or even in entering the Kingdom. Let a man who is already in the ministry become suddenly rich and the chances are exceedingly great that he will take sore throat and have to quit.

But in spite of all these heavy handicaps Moses did respond to God's call. He did turn aside from the easeful life of the shepherd to be the storm-center of his people for near a half a century. How do you account for him? There is but one answer, I repeat, and that is the answer of this old story. On the back side of the Midian desert one day he came face to face with God. Look at the picture. He is walking along old familiar paths. He has been there hundreds of times. As he watches his sheep he is thinking, as he has thought so often during these forty years, of his past, of his disappointed dreams and his blighted ambitions.

But chancing to lift his eyes, his attention is held by a rather strange sight on the mountain side. He sees a bush there that seems to be on fire. He watches it, expecting that almost instantly it will crumble into gray ashes. But to his amazement it burns on. The fire in the bush attracted his attention. The fact that the fire did not die excited his wonder.

How was it that God was able to speak to Moses through this burning bush? It was not because Moses was a particular favorite with God. God is just as willing to speak to you and me as he was to speak to him. He is speaking to us constantly, only we refuse to hear.

> "Earth's crammed with Heaven,
> And every common bush aflame with God.
> But only he who sees takes off his shoes.
> The rest stand round and pick blackberries."

God was able to speak to Moses in the first place because Moses in spite of all his trying experiences had not allowed himself to become a cynic. He had not lost the child heart. He could still appreciate the

ministry of surprise. He could still be made to clap his
hands in wonder. Many another man would have said:
"That burning bush seems altogether out of the ordinary. But I know it is ordinary after all, because
there is nothing new under the sun." And so saying
he would have passed on and have received no message.

In the second place Moses had not allowed himself
to become the bondslave of things. He was still free
enough to turn aside. "I will now turn aside," he says.
That is where many of us miss our vision. We will
not turn aside. We are too busy. Just as we are thinking of doing so, we are seized with a panic lest one of
our sheep should get away. Thus we hurry on, day
after day, taking no time to turn aside and hear God's
voice in the secret place of prayer, or to hear His voice
as He speaks through His Word, or to hear His voice
through the ministry of the Church.

Nor was Moses too tired to turn aside. Had you
been there you might have sighed and said: "Well, that
looks queer indeed, that burning bush, but I have followed the sheep so long that I am clean tired out. But
for this, I would turn aside and see." So we say
today. For instance, you say you work six days in
the week. On Sunday you just have to relax. This
you do by sleeping late, by doing your odd mending
and washing, by working in the garden or playing golf,
or painting your garage, or mending your auto, or
hurrying off to a picnic.

This you do because you are so tired. And if you
are forbidden to rest by these very charming methods
you go to the movies. Of course the movies have to
be open on Sunday because that is the only time that
the laboring folks have to go. And yet the day laborers

in my neighborhood quit work about four o'clock and have from then to midnight to attend six days in a week. What somniferous lies we tell ourselves!

Moses turned aside. Not only did he turn aside, but he turned aside reverently. Had he turned aside to subject this bush to candid criticism, had he blustered up to take its leaves to the laboratory, I do not think he would have heard anything. A spirit of irreverence will put out the fire for you everywhere. If you have no reverence for the truth you will not find it. If you have no reverence for the Word of God it will have no message for you. If you have no reverence for Jesus Christ, He will likely be to you "as a root out of dry ground, with no form nor comeliness."

Reverence is the doorway to knowledge. How did Huxley learn science? He sat down before her, he tells us, as a little child. He approached science reverently and science told him her secrets. Had he approached Jesus Christ in the same spirit he would have been as great a saint as he was a scientist. Let us cultivate reverence. Let us pray more earnestly the first petition of the Lord's prayer: "Hallowed be thy name." For this is almost a lost virtue. Well did Irvin Cobb say that if we were to examine the bump of reverence on the average man's head we would find it to be a dent.

Moses, you see, still had the child heart. He was still able to turn aside. He was reverent. Therefore God could speak to him. And what did He say through this undying fire that flamed in the bush? He told Moses that the secret of staying power was in Himself. That this bush should burn was not so wonderful, but that it should keep on burning was only to be accounted for by the power of God within it. Moses at once began to see his own failure in a new light. He himself had once been on fire. He himself once glowed with a fiery hatred against slavery and oppression. But where was the fire now? Gone out long ago and in his heart today were only dust and ashes.

Why had this fire that had once burned so fiercely in the heart of Moses gone out? It had not gone out because freedom had ceased to be desirable for the children of Israel. It had not gone out because the land of promise had ceased to exist. It had not gone out because righteousness was no longer a precious treasure. Moses had quit struggling, but this was not his reason for doing so.

Nor had Moses quit because the bondage of his people had ceased to be a galling and bitter thing. Slavery was just as tragic and just as damning after forty years as it was on that distant day when he had struck his one blow against it. It had lost none of its hatefulness, none of its power to wreck and to ruin. He had not ceased to burn, then, against wrong because wrong had ceased to exist or had become less wrong.

Nor are these your reasons. Where, may I ask, are the enthusiasms of your earlier years? How comes it that you have not struck a blow in behalf of right and against wrong since you came to this city? How is it that you have ceased to glow with enthusiasm for righteousness? How is it that you have ceased to burn with indignation against wrong? It is not because right is any less right. It is not because sin is any less hideous and damning. Sin is just as terrible today as it was yesterday, just as awful as when Jesus hung on the nails in His grim battle against it.

Nor had Moses ceased to burn for any reasons that

he was probably accustomed to give to himself. He had not quit, for instance, for lack of appreciation. It is true that his people had not appreciated him. It is also true that it is dreadfully hard to work without appreciation. I need it and you need it. But while appreciation is desirable it is not an absolute necessity. A word of praise may make our day seem brighter. It may make our load seem lighter and our climb up the hill seem less difficult. But if that word is not spoken we must still carry our burden and still continue our upward climb.

The task that Moses undertook forty years ago was a very difficult task, but that was not the real reason why he quit. The stupidity of his people, their unwillingness to be free, these things were very discouraging. They were very depressing, but that should not have been sufficient to turn him from his task. They would not have been sufficient but for this fundamental lack. He lacked what the bush had—the presence of God.

Watch him as he goes to that one fleeting effort. On whom is he depending as he strikes the Egyptian dead at his feet? He is counting on himself and on the loyalty of his people. God is not in the task. There is no "Lo, I am with you" ringing in his soul. He has no sense of a commission from God. When the jeerer asks him, "Who made you a prince and a judge over us?" he has no answer. He is merely vexed and greatly embarrassed.

Now it is not easy to stay at a hard task without a sense of the divine presence. It is not easy to keep going unless you feel yourself sent. It is God realized in your own life that gives you staying power. It is God seen in your task that makes most trying and difficult work possible and even beautiful. That nurse toiling at her exhausting work has the secret.

> "Oh, how could I serve in the wards if the hope of the world
>   were a lie?
> How could I endure the sights and the loathsome smell of
>   disease
> But that He said, 'Ye do it for me when ye do it for these.'"

With this vision Moses would never have made this same tragic mistake. During these forty desert years he has died to his own self-esteem. "Who am I," he says, "that I should deliver Israel?" Then God speaks to him. "Certainly, I will be with thee." It is not what you are but what God is. God can use the weakest of instruments. He can even speak through a dry bush. It is not so much in the sword as the hand that wields the sword.

God longed to go with Moses forty years ago, but He could not because Moses would not let Him. Moses did not feel that he needed Him. Moses was sufficient for the task himself. God cannot go with you unless you make room for Him. It is only those who feel their own utter insufficiency that have this promise: "Certainly, I will be with thee."

Armed now with the divine presence and fortified by a sense of commission, Moses sets himself to his task. A lone man with a shepherd's staff in his hand, he goes to invade the mightiest nation in the world. But he goes with the consciousness of the divine presence. He goes with the conviction that he is sent. When they ask him this time who sent him, he will not be dumb and ashamed. God has supplied him with an answer. "Tell them that I AM has sent you. Tell them that you have met your Master face to face and that He has sent you. And I will give you a mouth and a wisdom that they cannot resist."

The opposition of forty years ago was as a grain of sand to a world in comparison with the opposition that he met upon his second effort. But he never faltered. He was opposed by his enemies. He was opposed by his friends. Members of his own household turned against him. It seems that never was there another crowd so unreasonable, so full of pettiness and stupid criticism as the one with which he had to deal. Difficulties were everywhere. But we read of him this fine word: "He endured." How magnificent is that. Men misunderstood him, but he endured. People failed to appreciate him, but he endured. They criticized him unreasonably and unjustly, but he endured. At times he made no progress, but he endured. What is his secret? "He endured as seeing him who is invisible." He was sustained by the power of the God who had revealed himself to him through the burning bush.

I was just reading recently an interesting article in the *American Magazine,* entitled, "Why I Quit the Ministry." This man had quit for the very commonplace reason that his salary was so meager. He saw no way to educate his family, etc. In fact he made his reasons for quitting very clear, but he left his reasons for entering the ministry as dim as the shadow of a dream. In fact, the only reason that he became a preacher was because he overheard a good old saint say on one occasion that he was a fine boy and ought to preach. Entering the ministry for such a flimsy reason, no wonder it took no very colossal reason to force him to quit. No wonder the fire of his own kindling went out so easy. It is only God who gives us power to endure. "Even the youth shall faint and be weary, and the young men shall utterly fall, but they that wait upon the Lord shall renew their strength."

And now God is saying to you what He said to Moses: "Come, now I will send thee to Pharaoh." Every man is born into the world with a Pharaoh on his hands. Have you ever found yours? Have you ever met yours and fought him till he set his slaves free? Have you battled with him till his corpse has been left sprawled upon the seashore? Have you found your task and are you in the strength of God undertaking to do it?

I am not telling you where your Pharaoh is. I am not telling you just what particular mission God has given to you, but this I know. It is the part of helping and not of hindering. It is the part of ministering and not of being ministered unto. It is the part of working and not of idling. It is the part of playing the game and not of standing upon the side lines and criticizing.

"Now I will send thee." God wants you now. If you are an old body, he wants the last day of your life. If you are a child He wants you from your cradle to your grave. "Now I will send thee." If you put yourself in His hands and go with the sense of His presence you will not go in vain. Life becomes transfigured with light and with victory for that man who can look up from his duty, whether large or small, and say: "To this end was I born and for this cause came I into the world, that I might do this bit of work for God." May you have this blessed conviction from this day forward.